For Anne & Mike,
favorit people
British Columbia
Aug, 04
Charles

Read "A bear
Encounter" p. 18

At the River's Edge

At the River's Edge

LESSONS LEARNED IN A LIFE OF FLY FISHING

Jerry Kustich

Illustrations by Al Hassall

Jerry Kustich

West River Publishing

Published by
West River Publishing
P.O. Box 15
Grand Island, NY 14072

Portions of "Dream Keepers" and "Winter Song" appeared in *Fly Fisherman*
and *Montana Outdoors*, respectively. These pieces are reprinted with permission.

Special thanks to Valerie Haig-Brown and frater M. Charles Brant, erm. for
permission of material used in "Bear Encounter."

Excerpt from "There But for Fortune" written by Phil Ochs © Barricade Music
(ASCAP) administered by ASCAP Music Corp. appears with permission in "But for
Fortune."

Quote from *The Earth is Enough* by Harry Middleton in "Winter Song" appears
with permission from ING Literary, New York, NY.

Excerpt from *Trout Fishing in America* by Richard Brautigan appears in "The Caddis
Cure." Copyright © by Richard Brautigan. Reprinted by permission of Houghton
Mifflin Company/Seymore Lawrence. All rights reserved.

Quote from *A Sand County Almanac* by Aldo Leopold appears in "New Frontier"
with permission from Oxford University Press.

Excerpt from *Trout Magic* by Robert Traver appearing in "At the River's Edge"
reprinted by permission of the Estate of John D. Voelker and the John D. Voelker
Foundation.

Printed in the United States of America

First edition

10 9 8 7 6 5 4 3 2

Cataloging-in-Publication Data

Kustich, Jerry.
   At the river's edge : lessons learned in a life of
fly fishing / Jerry Kustich ; illustrations by Al
Hassall. -- 1st ed.
   p. cm.
   ISBN 0-9633109-2-5

   1. Fly fishing--Anecdotes. I. Title.

SH456.K87 2002   799.1'24
              QBI02-200489

To Debra:
For the patient support on an uncharted journey

Foreword

Ever wonder what it would be like to live the life of a full time fisherman? Well, Jerry lives that life. It is a life of purpose and passion—a powerful love affair with fish and fishing. Whether he casts his line across water or upon paper, he is forever fishing. Jerry's works reflect this love wholeheartedly. Like a King Arthur of the fishing world, rod, pen, and tongue are his Excalibur, forever seeking truth, spreading the message, pursuing bliss, and making peace within and without. Fishing is his life, the river his Holy Grail. His stories are what he has fully and truly experienced in his quest. I laughed, cried, relived my past and renewed my own love of the search as I read them.

Jerry has been at my right hand for many years. We have fished a world of water together, real and imagined. But my thoughts always return to Jerry as the "glue monkey," certainly a title of endearment. Our bamboo shop is a place where one day a week we team up for the gluing session—a tediously demanding ritual of crafting a split cane rod. Jerry spreads the glue over the six bamboo strips, then passes them to Jeff (the wrapping monkey) for pressure wrapping with string, and lastly I (the torque monkey) take the torque out of them before hanging the pieces in a heated cabinet for a number of months. The whole process is a foot tiring, repetitive affair that keeps our hands and eyes occupied, but our tongues and ears free. The end product is much more than a glued up section of bamboo. Great and unusual conversation is a valued by-product as well. Inhibitions seem to drop away during a repetitive process. It's strange how hard work can do that. But it is within this spirited team setting that we "cracker barrel" our problems, ideas, and fishing tales.

These days have become special, anticipated gatherings for us. In Jerry's book, all or parts of each of his stories were once verbalized during a gluing session. He is a wonderful storyteller. There are many spoken and unspoken understandings between us. The mumbled "dreaded tape" comment from Jeff would signal to Jerry that he had missed a step while getting too worked up in a story he was telling or a point that he was trying to make. Appeasing the bamboo spirits is another big part of the process, so at times of a slip up Jerry would do 50 hails to the bamboo gods while burning an incense of sweet grass. Woe be it should we tempt the fate of the bamboo gods. But in the end, the bamboo spirits seem to bless us all with much wisdom.

At the River's Edge reflects this wisdom. These stories are rich in truth about the fishing experience, but they are about more than fishing. Fishing is a means that keeps Jerry in touch with living life fully, keeping body and soul together. He has skillfully woven life's many colorful threads into a storied tapestry of what he has experienced. At the river's edge he has found the love of a woman, the loyalty of a friend, the companionship of a pet, a voice for those who have no voice, the mystical encounter, and the words to convey all this—along with much more. Reading these accounts is like the ever-changing nature of water, where I found myself bumping the river's edge of sorrow and joy, moving through life's currents with humility, honesty, and humor. They caught and released me. As a keen observer of life's wondrous and many details, Jerry blends all this into a book that honors the long legacy left by other writers of the fishing life—some 15,000 strong.

These stories are skillfully arranged. They took me from the calm quiet main stream waters, ever wondering around the bend, up side tribs, and then into the noisy headwaters (of his heart and mind). What you read is a little of his fishing exploits, but more the bittersweet experiences of his life's journey—the leaky waders part of life. Fishing for Jerry has become a rite of passage. Fish and rivers are his totem and spirit guides. He has stayed true to his calling. His work, a creative, beautiful wellspring of what he has lived and learned, reflect the old saying: "It's not what you do that matters, but the spirit you put into it."

I get a flood of thoughts and feelings realizing the huge emotional investment I have made, Jerry too, in some 50 years of fishing for each of us. Rivers and water, nature and wildness talk to my spirit, meeting an innate need I strongly believe we all share. Jerry has taken the proverbial journey into the desert seeking the waters of truth and life. His book shares with us what he has learned and valued during those 50 years of the journey.

I might add that Jerry's book of stories also keeps alive what John Voelker's (a.k.a. Robert Traver) *Trout Magic* and *Trout Madness*, and Roderick Haig-Brown's *A River Never Sleeps* spoke to about the fishing life and all its many experiences. These two heroes of Jerry would be proud of his book, and his fishing life, as am I.

As I write this on September 11, 2001, a dark, sad day in the history of the world, I realize that I will be fishing more, and I pray that more people do the same. The peace, patience, and tolerance fishing teaches are its important gifts. To be cleansed and uplifted by the wonders and magic of the angling experience... More than ever, I will be encouraging and showing others to the river's edge, especially my family. "Wade the rivers and get their good tidings, for your troubles will drop away like autumn leaves." (adapted from the writings of John Muir)

Glenn Brackett
September 11, 2001

Introduction

Sitting here in the bookstore, surrounded by tomes of literature representing an infinity of thoughts and ideas, I look for the inspiration to write a few magical lines to entice you, the reader, to continue on with the pieces contained within these covers. Sometimes outdoor stories are merely what they appear, and sometimes they cross into another dimension. In an age when so many are searching for something, I have found that the mere act of involvement with nature can open windows—to the heart, and perhaps, even to the soul. Whether it be hiking, canoeing, cross-country skiing, bird watching, fishing or so many other quiet outdoor activities, a devotion to the natural world can awaken a spirit deep within, perhaps evoking the vestige of a time when the human being was closer to the rhythms of Mother Earth. For some, fly fishing provides this link; and for me, specifically, what emerges is what I call a "fly philosophical" approach to a meaningful existence.

Years ago, I took up playing guitar as the "in thing" during the turmoil of the sixties. At a time when Bob Dylan, Phil Ochs, Tim Buckley, to mention a few, touched many with songs of passion and deep reflection, these artists also moved me to play their music and, subsequently, to write my own. Later, when I traded my guitar for a fly rod, I still found the urge to write, but this time it was to link the outdoor experience with the deeper realities of life. In a world that is getting more and more shrinked-wrapped with asphalt, the opportunity to connect with all the natural world has to offer is steadily diminishing. There are some who likewise believe mankind will never be able to exchange a life encased in concrete without losing that which is vital to the human spirit. Thus, I believe, it is the role of the outdoor story to perpetuate why this elemental bond is so important. Not only through fly fishing do I remain immersed in what is significant, but it is also the fly fishing experience that arouses my power of creativity. And because creativity is a potent elixir, it is my interpretation of the world I would like to share as a possible key to unlock the door leading to a peaceful and contented existence.

A favorite minstrel of mine from bygone times, the late Harry Chapin, once wrote long, lyrical stories of people and life put to song. How he could pack so much detail into each selection was most intriguing. In fact, I feel his premature death motivated me to be a storyteller. So after several decades of rambling the roads less taken, the pieces in this book have finally come together. These works represent my attempt to a write an album of sorts, with a theme based on observations made through the eyes of a fly angler. The stories are true, and they are mine, but the music is whatever you choose to bring to them.

America the Beautiful: A Prelude

From where I live in Montana, it's a long drive to the Klamath River. There is really no route that makes sense either. But the final choice is usually determined by how the stars are aligned on the day of my departure, and on this particular trip the heavens pointed to Missoula. So off I headed. Once there, the subsequent journey traces a memory-filled blacktop to Lewiston, Idaho, via the Lochsa and Clearwater Rivers. After that, it is an arduous trek through the hot, parched Palouse Region of Washington State to Walla Walla. The rustic community of Umatilla follows, and then it is the Columbia River Gorge that offers a visual respite in the form of trapped water stilled by a series of hydro-dams. Sometime, well into the second day, Bend, Oregon, breaks up the tedious excursion. And after a brief stop charged by a serious jolt of Starbucks, Klamath Falls appears within hours. There the tactical decision is made on how best to negotiate the final few hundred miles that offers the most likely opportunity to intercept the "half-pounder" run on the lower Klamath. This occurs on the morning of the third day near the Northern California coast.

The term "half-pounder" is colloquial for a strain of small steelhead that is quite often larger than eight ounces. This unique variety of sea-run rainbow runs up a mere handful of coastal rivers in Northern California and Southern Oregon starting in late August. As long as anyone can remember, this run has always existed. And though a big half-pounder usually goes about three pounds or so, in a good season quantity makes up for the lack of size.

For years I have had a fascination with this run, and occasionally the opportunity to fish it is woven between so many other options. Like this year, for example. There were big fish in the Clearwater near Lewiston, but I drove past them. The Deschutes was loaded with steelhead as well. But I drove past them too. For some reason I am drawn to the stunning Klamath— its beauty and its wonderful little fish. And though I can't deny the ironic satisfaction derived from heading toward California while a procession of SUVs loaded with fly gear head from that state to the Rockies, my delight goes much deeper than that. Ever since my childhood years in Western New York, I have had this burning desire to fish for steelhead on the West Coast. Still caught up in this dream, I chase these elusive piscatory symbols of survival whenever I can.

I know. To have such a yen for steelhead while living in Montana seems counter intuitive—at least on the surface. But during late fall, fish that have entered the Columbia River only a few months earlier arrive in Idaho's upper Salmon River just one hundred and twenty-five miles from my Montana home. Although many of them are hatchery fish, a small percentage are wild. Imagine! These wild steelhead were spawned somewhere in the Salmon, survived the many stages of growth until becoming nine inch smolts, and then, with a determination that defies all odds, they head to the ocean. One thousand miles and eight dams later, some actually make it to saltwater to swim with the seals and so many other predators. After two years in the Pacific, the ones that haven't been eaten or netted in the high seas return to the Columbia to embark upon another impossible journey. Dodging

Native American nets along the way and finding all the fish ladders that take them back up over eight dams, the preposterous occurs. Every year a few wild fish survive to swim through the water that is only two hours from where I live.

In the mid 80s I happened to catch one of these wild beauties in the presence of friend and former Idaho Fish and Game biologist Mel Reingold. Upon its release, he wrung his hands in reverence. After a brief silence, his insightful words radiated wisdom that should be considered throughout the remainder of time: "Mankind has done all in its power to eliminate this great fish from its native habitat, yet we haven't been able to do it yet. There is no creature on earth that possesses the spirit of a steelhead—especially a wild Salmon River steelhead. It is a beautiful fish that desires—with all its might—to live within the special waters of the earth's most breathtaking reaches. And what's more, its obsessive effort to cling to all that is pure reminds each and every one of us of the absolute need for these beautiful places in our lives. One thousand miles down, one thousand miles back, and you catch it. What a fish!"

Mel's words were braised into my psyche then, and they inspire my pursuit to this day. But it was only after a six week sojourn to Kamchatka a few years back that my awe for this species elevated to sublime heights. In this wondrous Lost World of genetically untainted salmonids, the land and water held many insights. As if hot-lined directly from a transcended source, voices in the winds of wilderness seemed to reveal a simple truth about the relationship between man and steelhead. Because harmony and balance is essential for its survival, a steelhead is like a tuning fork. Where it still exists, a wild steelhead represents all that is right with the natural realm. And though the whole of mankind doesn't yet realize the implications, in my solitude it became clear that the human spirit can not possibly survive the long haul without protecting the wild places that support indomitable creatures like the steelhead. This was a powerful message derived from a magical land.

The clarion call from the West Coast rings with the desperation of immediacy. Even the steelhead transplanted to the Great Lakes in the late 1800s raise awareness to the cause. For me, visiting these fish where they live has become an essential force in my life. I figure if a steelhead can swim one thousand miles to touch me in nearby Idaho, I can certainly drive a thousand miles now and then to encounter the many variations of its world.

So standing in the Klamath on the second morning of my arrival, everything seemed perfect. The fog hung in low stillness, and the placid surface broke only with the occasional silver glint of a small steelhead. Just knowing these wild creatures were swimming by the spot where I was standing elevated my entire being. In the peacefulness of the moment there was absolutely no awareness of the horror that was taking place at the exact moment across the continent. Lost in a stream of content contemplation, the mood was interrupted by an older angler calling out to me in mid cast. Standing on the shoreline with a spinning rod in his hand, he didn't look familiar. As he signaled to me and shouted once again, I waded close enough to hear what he had to say.

" Have you heard the news?" The stranger asked in a somber mood.

Although I didn't know what could possibly be so important to disturb a fine morning of fishing, my heart pounded in response to the foreboding tone of his question. Then, in the most terrible story one would ever dare to imagine, he related the grim events unfolding on that very morning of September 11, 2001.

For a brief second the river stopped flowing. There is no way words of such tragic magnitude could be comprehended. Staring at the angler, I mumbled an incoherent something, and then headed back to my vehicle in a state of overwhelming shock. On the radio Dan Rather's grim report confirmed this absurdity of diabolical proportions. I closed my eyes. Normally, I find enlightenment at the river's edge, but on this occasion there was only a sense of loss. In truth I was afraid to approach the river again fearing that somehow knowledge so grotesque could taint such tranquility. At once I took off my waders, packed my rod, and headed home to my wife.

My mind emerged from a numbing state of protective retreat on the second day of the return trip. The rage and anger finally subsided to a bearable level amidst a moving rendition of "America the Beautiful" playing on NPR. Around the nation, heavy hearts burdened by insufferable sorrow shadowed any attempt to deal adequately with the fearful implications of this shameless attack on all that is civilized. In an effort, perhaps, to cope with the intolerable in terms of personal relevance, my mind drifted to a lesson garnered from the world of steelhead. Like these magnificent fish, now more than ever we humans must cling to all that is pure as well, to embrace all the beauty that we possibly can—as if our existence depends on it. For without the sanctuary of beautiful places in our lives, there is really no hope that our collective soul will survive such ugliness and evil. Plain and simple! America the beautiful, I thought—a patriotic call of a different sort to reverently preserve all places of calm and beauty in the memory of those who died so needlessly. May the seeds of love and kindness grow from these places, and may a better world emerge for all creatures inhabiting the Earth.

I drove in silence. It was a long, sad journey home.

A Bear Encounter

"It is in the history of civilizations that conservationists are always defeated, boomers always win, and the civilizations always die. I think there has never been, in any state a conservation government, because there has never yet been a people with sufficient humility to take conservation seriously. This is natural enough. No man is intimately concerned with more than his lifetime, comparatively few men concern themselves with more than a fraction of that time; in the last analysis all governments reflect the concerns of the people they govern, and most modern democratic governments are more deeply concerned with some brief, set term of office than anything else. Conservation means fair and honest dealing with the future, usually at some cost to the immediate present. It is simple morality, with little to offset the glamour and quick material rewards of the North American deity: Progress."

Measure of the Year, 1950
Roderick L. Haig-Brown

Empty rivers. When I drive through the state of Washington, that's all I see. Sure, there are still remnant fish here and there, some token runs of beleaguered steelhead and salmon hold on despite a myriad of reasons to vanish entirely, but these insipid ribbons now represent the squandering of a society which seems to have lost touch with such matters. To encounter so many beautiful rivers devoid of a rich heritage in a region once defined by its bountiful resources can still cut through the numbness of today's overwhelming indifference. As images of what-should-be swim through the rage of the few who care, these waters of lifelessness engulf those who wade in search of glimpses from the past, the dreams that once fed fancies of youthful exuberance not too many years ago. One has to wonder whether the price of progress is worth the cost. Though man's ingenuity has the ability to proceed into the future without sacrificing the biodiverse settings which surround him, the lack of concern for this basic fundamental principle could be a flaw that one day proves fatal. Empty rivers. That's all I see.

I still explore, and will continue to do so, for waters of significance. And though Vancouver Island has not been immune to the same influences prevalent in the state to its south, I look there to connect to a man to whom we all should have paid more attention in the past. Roderick Haig-Brown's home still stands on the south bank of the Campbell River less than a mile upstream from where it enters the Strait of Georgia, the inside passage between the Island and the mainland. The man was a pioneer conservationist in an era that took a dim view of such beliefs (not that the times have changed much since then). And the river was once a great one, but its life was cut short by a dam; few fish return there anymore. These days, Haig-Brown's house has been restored, and the property is now a protected provincial heritage site where educational programs and tours, along with seminars, workshops, and retreats, are regularly scheduled to address topics such as conservation, fisheries, and natural history. That these hallowed grounds preserve the life and spirit of the man who may well have been the first writer ever to address the controversial conservation issues of his time is a credit to a province bent on perpetuating many of his concerns.

When fishing this region, I seek a window of enlightenment; I search for the door that opens to a realm of inspiration. If one is to carry on the torch of concern for our vanishing anadromous fish, it is essential to first find an ember. There is an undeniable presence along the rivers Haig-Brown once fished, and I long to hook into any kind of insight he may have left behind, lingering within some forgotten reach, before that opportunity vanishes too. Alongside these waters, perhaps there is something more. The Earth still remembers what has been lost in less than a century of development, for in terms of cosmic time, the change has occurred in but a tick. And if one listens closely, mournful cries, like a mother lamenting the death of a child, echo through the void. Though the forces of nature continue to speak, the truth of its message fades into the distance as our ability to listen gives way to the confusing cacophony of modern existence.

I once read a moving story written by Father Charles Alfred Edwin Brandt that reflects the simple substance of man's relationship to the Earth—especially in this part of the world. While fishing stories relate the essence of why many of us fish, this piece expressed the fusion of mind, soul, and body with an elemental unifying force sometimes found in the outdoor experience. It should be noted that Father Brandt is a renowned paper conservationist and restorer of old books. As a Director of the Haig-Brown Kingfisher Creek Society, he has been active in the maintenance of Haig-Brown's library. For this reason alone, I was interested in Charles's short story. Additionally, as an environmental conservationist, he has been quite active in projects designed to restore salmon runs to some of the Island's depleted rivers. Since the piece took place on the Campbell River, my imagination was captivated upon reading the first word.

In this tale, Charles had just hooked an enchanting wild Campbell River summer steelhead when he became aware of a strange presence on the shore behind him. From over his shoulder, he happened to notice what appeared to be a black bear blending into the bushes as it watched him fight the fish for a better part of an hour. But when the fight was over, the bear was gone. At the very moment he released the fish, however, he was alerted by a sound directly behind him. The noise which startled him, though, was caused by a big man dressed in black; in fact, this man was a friend, the local head of fisheries from the Ministry of Environment. Charles reasoned his friend was likely the "bear" he had observed. After exchanging congenial conversation, both men began to walk back to the parking lot. Following the head of fisheries up the steep trail at a comfortable distance, Charles still had a few questions to ask him about the coastal cutthroat project on the nearby Oyster River, an effort they each took very seriously. His inquiries could wait, he figured, until they got back to the vehicles. But when Charles got over the rise and into the parking area, his friend was gone. He did not hear him drive away, there hardly seemed time. Yet, there was no sign of him.

In the mythologies of the North Coast indigenous people, Charles went on to describe, they speak of a primordial age "when finite divisions between humans, animals and spirits had not yet been created, a time when humans could become animals by putting on skins, and animals could become humans by taking them off. Then everything was connected; earth, sky and land by beings who could pass through and among them. All was infused and penetrated by the Great Spirit." Present-day totem carvings, some prominently displaying the bear, keep the mythology alive. Because I desire to retrace some of Haig-Brown's footsteps and hope to be embraced by the primordial Great Spirit in the process, I read this unique story before every visit to Vancouver Island.

These days, I drive there occasionally to pursue sea-run cutthroats. Since I have always been impassioned by the variety of cutthroat subspecies found throughout the West, it has long been a goal to catch at least one of each in its native habitat. The sea-run cutthroat is a hearty fish that spends a portion of its life within the estuaries of the Pacific. In certain areas, particularly on Vancouver Island, populations of these fish have responded quite well to the restrictive measures enacted to restore their numbers. Usually, I catch sea-runs with a cumbersome 7 or 8 weight in the process of swinging flies for steelhead. The few available days were to be spent, instead, hunting this fine fish balanced with the proper gear. Haig-Brown once wrote that "the true sea-run cutthroat is a very special fish and makes very special fishing." Again, the words of the master guided my efforts. Sometimes it is too easy to get waylaid by the glamour of the steelhead; too often these little gems are either overlooked or merely taken for granted. For many reasons, I wanted to catch a sea-run cutthroat by choice, not by accident. And since the timing was just about right, I planned to spend one day fishing the Oyster River, mentioned in the Charles Brandt story, with the hopes of encountering just a few—while coming to grips with the reality that steelhead numbers on the Island's eastern shoreline were approaching all-time lows.

As the low light of dawn emerged through a foggy mist one day in late April, the lower pools of the Oyster near the waters of the Straight beckoned from the bridge crossing. This is a small river. Its water flows crystal clear, originating from the heart of the Island's glacial interior. A #8 rolled muddler was the fly pattern suggested by the local shop to match the salmon fry as these diminutive fish drifted toward the waters of the estuary at this time of year. In theory, coastal cutthroats should be well-tuned to this event. Furthermore, with a little luck, some sea-runs should be hanging in the lower reaches looking for a meal. Apparently the news was out, for on that tranquil morning, several silver beauties came to my offering. Not big, but feisty, these anadromous cutts seemed to exhibit the same vigor common to their larger salmonid relatives, especially on equipment scaled proportionally down to size. Given the objectives of this recent trip, I felt energized, absolutely wired to the reason behind the journey.

Later that afternoon, following the advice of a knowledgeable friend, I walked a few miles upstream along the public path that led to many pools. The plan was to fish from the restricted barrier, marking water closed to public angling for the protection of the fish, all the way back to the parking area. It would take an hour to get there. The hike was pleasant and reflective until the quiet buzz of nature was abruptly invaded by the irritating blast of two dirt bikes. Glued to the seats of these abrasive machines were a pair of late-teenage males. Appearing a bit guilty, they stopped to chitchat for a while. Though it never came up whether motorized vehicles were allowed on the path, the kids remained a bit edgy. While the engines revved, one offered a tidbit of encouragement based upon his limited fishing knowledge of the river. Then, in a cloud of dust and exhaust, they took off. As the noise delightfully dissipated up the trail, the ensuing silence was, to my dismay, short-lived. Ten minutes later the boys returned.

"There's a big black bear up there on the trail!" one exclaimed as they slowed to a complete stop. "We aren't going any farther."

Somewhat spooked, the other added, "I don't like bears." They both agreed it should be shot.

Surprised by the reaction of the two pseudo-macho adolescents, I could only imagine this was the mentality responsible for the dead bear my wife found last fall while she was walking along the Klamath River. Minus its paws, the mutilated carcass was subsequently left in the California sun to bake in symbolic testimony to wanton disrespect.

Questioning my sanity for moving on, the boys figured they had done their good deed by offering the warning. I thanked them, but privately I really thanked the bear for balancing nature, at least for the rest of the afternoon. Coming upon the exact spot on the path where it was obvious the boys had come to a screeching halt, I stopped to look and listen. Sure enough, substantial crunching in the dense undergrowth scarcely a forty-foot cast off the trail confirmed that something was out there. Assuming it was the bear, I decided not to tempt fate by dawdling. Onward I trudged.

There were still a good twenty minutes left before reaching the restricted water. Most of the walk to this point took place out of the Oyster's view. So a few hundred feet up from where the alleged bear was making noise in the woods, a side trail led to an observation point, and this proved to be a good place to see what I had been missing. There, the river is medium-sized, but recent rains gave it a bigger than normal appearance as it sliced a cool corridor through a forest of spruce and cedar. This is a piece of water that certainly could entice a contingent of faithful followers. At that point it possessed the distinct character common to many cutthroat waters throughout the West—very long, inviting runs with the right depth and broken surface separated by shallow, swift riffles. Although the best-looking section on this stretch would have to be fished from the other side, it was obvious, even from a distance, that crossing would be difficult. Though it was alluring, I was sure there had to be water upstream which didn't require wading to the opposite shore. As I admired this beautiful piece of cutthroat water while debating a strategy for the rest of the day, I detected movement. Then, at that exact moment, the big black bear appeared! Walking slowly out of the brush toward the tailout above the definitive hole upon which I was gazing, it swam effortlessly across to the other side. Like a huge dog, it shook the water off a rather large body and meandered confidently into the woods on a path which it apparently knew well. Immediately, Father Brandt's tale came to mind accompanied by the thrilling chill that comes from being touched briefly by a special moment.

As far as coincidences go, seeing the bear after recently rereading Charles Brandt's story was a fairly mild one. In the minds of many, it would hardly qualify. But my life has been defined by coincidences of one kind or another—some have been quite sensational. A few have even spooked potential relationships. A psychologist friend once told me he firmly believed that coincidences are merely random events that have the appearance of being significant, but occur only by pure, empirical chance. However, after working together for a year in Idaho's Selway-Bitterroot Wilderness, he admitted that I redefined his perception of the concept. There was no way, he concluded, that the regular unexplained events in my life could possibly be random.

I figure whatever this aberration is, it must have come from my mother. She believes strongly in a "reality beyond" that provides us with what we need, when we need it. Call it Kismet, Karma, Divine Intervention, Universal Force, etc., if you are plugged into this Power, the unexplained happens. For instance, several years ago my mother paid for a small amount of groceries with a twenty dollar bill at a time in my folks' life when twenty dollars was a lot of money. Distracted momentarily, it wasn't until she reached the parking lot that Mom realized the clerk neglected to include a ten dollar bill in her change. After attempting to rectify the mistake, she was very hurt—like anybody's honest mother would be—when the clerk accused her of lying. Needless to say, Mom had to accept the loss of ten hard earned dollars and move on. The very next day, Dad was removing Christmas lights from the front porch of our home in late March. As he kicked back a pile of old soggy leaves to establish solid footing for the ladder, he discovered, to his amazement, a wet, washed-out—but still usable—ten dollar bill partially hiding under the exposed earth. It had apparently been there for quite some time waiting for just the right moment to be discovered.

The way I see it, maybe a coincidence is a conduit to our primordial past when, as Father Brandt wrote, "finite divisions between humans, animals and spirits had not been created...everything was connected...all was infused and penetrated by the Great Spirit." Perhaps coincidences are a vestige of a sixth sense where instinct and inner voice fused primitive races to a keen awareness of natural forces for the purpose of physical and spiritual survival. There is no question that aboriginal peoples understood this dimension of oneness. For them, there was a fine line between life and death. In present-day terms, this is a difficult notion to comprehend. In a world of ingenious machinations, our ability to look within ourselves has become increasingly hindered by a myriad of fascinating distractions. As a consequence, it would seem that the modern version of humanity is destined to lose touch with the capacity to listen to Earth's rhythms, to no longer feel the power that our withering sixth sense once provided. Whatever it all means, I enjoy the speculation. So when my inner voice told me to follow the bear, I did.

The river was chest deep where the bear crossed, but the bottom was smooth and the gravel gripped my wading shoes like the caress of an old friend. The depth of flow dispersed the downstream push of water while the wading staff fashioned from a bleached-out, broken branch provided all the support needed to reach the other side. After a brief rest, I first walked downriver and proceeded to methodically fish through the lower third of the run. Although the water felt "fishy," there was no sign of a cutthroat. Preparing to trek back to the head of the pool, I stopped abruptly. The focus of my mission was interrupted by the distinct crackling of a creature walking down the path utilized by the bear less than one half-hour beforehand. Naturally assuming the bear had returned for an encore performance, I slipped quietly behind a willow, fumbled for the camera, and prepared to take an obligatory wildlife snapshot. Usually, when developed, such photos appear to be a dark, undefined lump of something on an otherwise boring print. This time, though, I was positioned nicely to actually shoot a great picture. But when the creature came into view, my initial feeling of disappointment was immediately displaced by a sense of surprise. Another coincidence? Maybe.

Perhaps the bear really did remove its skin. But when the elderly gentleman with a fly rod in hand stepped through the opening, I just stared as if suspended in a mystical state of mind. Again the Father Brandt story flashed as a possible explanation for the bear's transformation. The senior angler then gingerly ambled over the round river rock to the upper bend where I was headed.

In silence, still out of sight, I observed the man as he began to fish the water with the simplicity of an expert. Clad in a vintage vest, his patched waders properly understated his presence while his skillful casts delivered a fly with a distinct sense of purpose. Undoubtedly this fellow belonged there, and it was a fitting stroke of chance that I hadn't beat him to the spot. In an attempt not to startle him, I voiced a greeting from a distance. He smiled warmly as I approached, saying hello in the same gesture.

"You didn't see the bear, did you?" I asked and then continued without stopping, "About thirty minutes ago, it headed up the very path you just came down ."

"You don't say!" he replied with a chuckle. "Nope, didn't see him."

Since the camera was cocked and ready to shoot, I confided to him my disappointment that he wasn't the bear—but if he didn't mind, I'd take *his* picture instead. Chuckling once again, he pleasantly agreed to the offer.

After the photo shoot, we talked for quite a while. The man was a scholarly, gentle soul who knew a great deal about the local rivers. Asking him several questions relating to the coastal cutthroat, he filled in many blanks about their behavior and run timing. Although he had caught a very nice cutt upriver, he informed me that these fish just completed their spawn, so most had probably dropped back to the estuary with this last bump of rain. And though he detailed some good "holes" to sample immediately below our position, he concluded that the best opportunity at this time of year would be found in the lower pools, thus confirming my early-morning experience.

The conversation evolved to a serious discussion about the issues facing West Coast salmonid stocks. The man turned somber as he reflected upon the disintegration of the resource. Though he considered the coastal cutthroat a bright spot, the populations of native steelhead and coho, particularly on the Oyster, have declined dismally. His pain was clear as he described the way it used to be not too very long ago. He added that local sportsmen were trying to do something about the situation. Pointing to the nearby live rearing pens in the river, he extolled their efforts designed to help coho get a jump-start before heading down to the ocean. In fact, it was his turn to tend to the pens that day.

When I expressed my concern for this eroding resource along with a passionate drive to do something about it, he asked if I had yet visited the Haig-Brown house. The wise old angler was genuinely pleased to hear that I had recently spent a day there. He indicated that there was no better source of information for what I was attempting to do. It was then I realized that the bear had led me to what I was looking for all along—and this fine man seemed to be it. We continued to talk about empty rivers and Haig-Brown's concept of simple morality: that is, preserving the last of our wild salmonids for future generations at whatever cost to the immediate present, because it is simply the right thing to do.

"It is in the history of civilizations that conservationists are always defeated..." echoes the words of Haig-Brown through the nexus of time lost, and with predictable certitude, the cycle repeats. The trend he observed years ago continues, as if mankind is doomed to be incapable to do anything about it. Specious politicians make promises in order to get elected with no commitment whatsoever to matters of nature. Even those most concerned with fishery resources—sportsmen, biologists, commercial interests—can't agree upon any plan that makes long-lasting sense. And while "progress" continues to suck the lifeblood from the veins of the world that once was, I find it difficult to look into the eyes of today's youth knowing it is their heritage we have laid to waste. Conservation! That's all it would have taken.

It was a beautiful afternoon. Likely, we both felt the pull of the river when I sensed that it was time to move on. Compelled by the need to enter the silence of my own space, I expressed my sincere thanks for his shared knowledge. I gave the gentleman one of my cards before heading down river, but that prompted another brief discussion about rod building and bamboo. Finally, I said good-bye.

"And by the way," I added, somewhat embarrassed while reaching out to shake his hand, "I apologize for not asking your name before this."

"Oh! That's okay," he said with a twinkle in his eye. "My name is Charles Brandt."

In an instant, the consideration of coincidence, random event, destiny, or even fate flashed through my mind. Or maybe this was simply a portal in time back to when human, animal, and spirit were one, a primitive age when nature was life. Whatever it may have been, for a fleeting, unique moment, everything significant converged into one notable experience. Nothing made sense, yet somehow everything did.

Reflecting upon the bear and the powerful force it symbolized in Native cultures, I walked down to the next run. And just before casting my fly, I looked back upriver.

The man was gone.

Finding a Story

Don't ask me why, but I've always wanted to be a writer. Then again, I always wanted to be a fireman, or even a baseball player. But since nature and fishing have been a force in my life since childhood, being an outdoor writer makes some kind of sense—at least at my age. Not that I have any proclivity for that sort of thing, but this mere technicality doesn't stop others from filling the pages of our favorite fishing magazines with print issue after issue. And there's no lack of aspiring Ted Truebloods either. Not long ago, I read that Nick Lyons reviewed over four hundred fly fishing manuscripts during the previous year. "These days everyone thinks they are writers" was the one comment of his that stood out among the rest. What the heck, add one more to the list! I went to a Catholic school, and, by God, I learned about subjects and predicates, nouns and verbs; I even learned how to spell them without getting my knuckles cracked. A gerund. Now that's a different story, but I try not to use any of them anyway. How the same dictionary of words can produce the works of Dickens or Hemingway on the one hand and the drivel, say, of Rush Limbaugh on the other is one thing I don't yet understand.

Apparently, you don't have to be particularly talented these days; you just have to have an audience.

What to write. Now that's a problem. Although outdoor pieces range from the poetic to the humorous and everywhere in between, there has been the inclination in most outdoor magazines to take the genteel, middle-of-the-road approach. But it's no secret, I am not a happy guy. When I look at the environment, I want to give a toxic enema to the legions of modern-day Visigoths responsible for all the residual crap every one of us has to deal with on the planet. And while the same irresponsible elite sit their complacent behinds on some beach in a place like the Bahamas, breathing in the last of the fresh air and bad-mouthing the environmental extremists fighting for issues like clean water, they also propagandize the so-called "liberals" as if they were the last vestige of a communist plot to overthrow the venerable American Way of Life. Call me weak, but the present-day tendency to rape and pillage our land for profit while leaving future generations to grovel for the few environmental crumbs that drop through the floorboards of progress leaves me a bit queasy. Needless to say, many of my first works were thinly veiled, subliminal attempts to sway the readership to pick up placards and fight the fight against this hopeless doom we all have been responsible in some degree for creating. After my wife reviewed a piece or two, she concluded that the only person who could possibly appreciate such existential angst was Albert Camus—and he's dead. And besides, she added, I was only preaching to the converted. It was then I concluded that the need for a fresh angle, a revitalized perspective, was in order. While outdoor articles can definitely make a point, they should also be about something like, well, fish or other related topics.

Reading a short story by Scott Waldie in the mid-eighties about an old man catching the fish of a lifetime on the Big Hole River piqued my interest in this genre. So much can be said within the context of a story, and the spirit of that special piece captured the true substance and mystique of the outdoor experience. At the same time, it inspired an inner yearning to find for myself an avenue of similar self-expression. While the "where to" or "how to" article has its place, the fishing story addresses the wherefores, and that is the real reason I fish. The study of other authors led to an enlightening conclusion: if only I could capture the wit of John Gierach, the insight of John Voelker a.k.a. Robert Traver, the prose of Nick Lyons, the consciousness of Roderick Haig-Brown, and the spirit of Scott Waldie, I would have it made. Sure! While I'm at it, I might as well wish for the Army Corps of Engineers to tear down eight dams so that wild steelhead and salmon can resurrect themselves from the brink of extinction and return once again to the Columbia River. (There I go again— politically heated rhetoric!) In other words, it doesn't hurt to think big.

About the time Scott's story appeared in *Fly Fisherman* magazine, I wandered into his Twin Bridges fly shop for the first time. Since I came off as an esoteric, ex-hippie trout geek trying to get his act together in this small corner of Brown-Trout-R-Us, Montana, we hit it off from the first exchange of words. In fact, he couldn't have been more sincere, a quality gone the way of the great auk these days. Although his demeanor was that of the respectable fly shop owner, the tattered pictures on the wall hidden beneath the happy-face-fish-holding-photos divulged his subcultured past. Somewhat introspective and intensely reserved, Scott's personality had a withdrawn edge about it. You got the impression right from the start that he'd rather be a hermit in a far off cabin writing volumes about the stories that were flashing through his mind.

As our pasts unfolded, it seemed we were both of the Brotherhood still searching for the ideals of the late sixties as if they were the elusive lost ark of truth and light. Scott had a certain down-to-earth quality about him, as well. As I found out over the years, he would do anything for anyone in need. And since he had a low tolerance for the superficial, his friends were honest and true. In between their frequent visits, it wasn't unusual to find Scott banging away on his typewriter keys to the tunes of Bob Dylan and other social rebels of that "turned-on" generation when he wasn't answering phone calls or selling the occasional Yuk Bug. His golden lab, Annie, was always by his side. When I wasn't fishing or working at my newly acquired Winston Rod job, I eventually found myself spending a few days every summer at his shop peddling flies to tourists while making long-winded small talk (my trademark) to anybody and everybody who wanted to discuss anything that had to do with trout. In fact, whether they wanted to or not, we *would* talk trout.

For some reason, there was always something glamorous about this writing stuff. The allure dated back to an early life addiction to *Mad* magazine. Even in the movies, when the handsome star described his overtly obscure career as that of being a writer, the very concept of this cryptic occupation ran chills up my spine. Scott, however, portrayed a more realistic image of the profession. It seemed that a writer actually spent a lot of time writing. So much for the glamour of the movies! I couldn't even stand composing a five-page term paper in college. I suppose if it had to do with the significance of the Royal Wulff instead of dissertations related to Jean-Paul Satre's wrenching insights into the confusions emanating from the deplorable depths of the human condition, I may have had a different attitude. Still, I just wanted to write one good outdoor story.

Hanging on the wall of Scott's Four Rivers Fishing Company were two huge fish: a brown and a rainbow. Although these were the trout of dreams, as it turned out they were not quite what they seemed. Scott found the ten pound rainbow floating dead in the Big Hole during the late seventies. No sense leaving a nice fish like that to go to waste, he reasoned, so why not hang it on the wall. The other was a fourteen pound brown caught on the Jefferson River in the mid-seventies by Charlie Thomas, the inveterate Montana old-timer who loved to haunt the local waters with chunks of sucker meat cut from the hide of these big-lipped bottom feeders and dangled from the business end of twenty pound test spinning line. After hunting Charlie down one day, we talked for hours about that "wall hanger." He was convinced that sucker meat was the only way to catch a fish of that magnitude. I wondered out loud whether he thought there were any more like that one in the Jeff. He scratched his chin thoughtfully before he answered. Since that was the biggest fish of his sucker-meat career, and since he was over seventy, "darn few" was his predictable, but thoughtful, reply. Taking a fish like that one on a fly—what a story that would make! Even an amateur like myself could smell an angle in there somewhere. Those two icons adorned the walls of Four Rivers for years, no doubt evoking the incantations of the many faithful who had often stood in their presence to pay homage.

Scott and I would regularly get into conversations about big fish, but only because I would push the subject. Being a data-oriented, self-appointed fishologist with a background rooted in natural sciences, I was always interested in exact and precise facts. I wanted to know the accurate length of a nice fish—what it took, how it fought, the time of day, if it was cloudy, and so on. Scott, on the other hand, was more from the Gestalt school of thought, and usually spoke in terms of vague generalities. Of course, he was also a guide. When I asked him once about the veracity of all the twenty-inch fish claimed to be caught daily by everyone passing through the doors, he just laughed.

One day, in the course of our normal chit-chat, Scott casually interjected, "Caught Spot again the other day." The songs of Little Feat played in the background.

"Spot who?" I curiously asked, not at all prepared for what I was about to hear.

Acting genuinely surprised, he queried, "You mean I have never told you about Spot?"

Apparently, I had to earn a certain degree of trust before this story was to ever come out of the closet.

Scott then proceeded to fill me in on the details. Summed up concisely, Spot was a big ole brown trout that dwelled in a depression under a particular clump of willows on the Big Hole River near his home. Scott had tangled with this brute several times over the years. Although he only landed Spot a couple times, he was always able to get a rise from the big fish in the form of a boil or a grab on several other occasions.

"He was twenty-five inches this time." Scott's tone was nonchalant, but my eyes bulged like a kid's on Christmas day when he delivered that news.

"But how do you know it was the same fish?" This was the first of many questions I tossed his way that afternoon. Excitement accented the feverish pitch of my voice.

"By the distinctive scar on its back, it looks like a big spot." He added, "Must be an old wound from a heron."

What a concept—striking up a personal relationship with a veteran brown trout in a secret place on a favorite river! Although I was surprised that he had never told me about Spot before, that was the kind of thing Scott thought wasn't that important. Noting my enthusiasm, Scott suggested that I talk to Doc Beithon, for he had a couple of pet browns also, and they were hidden away somewhere on the Beaverhead. The Band then ushered me out the door whistling to the tune of "Up on Cripple Creek."

Doc Beithon, the definitive country doctor, moved to Montana primarily for the fishing in the early seventies. If that didn't inspire confidence, the picture of the forty-four inch Clearwater steelhead placed conspicuously on the shelf in his office surely would. During any official office call, the conversation would always turn to the joys of steelheading. Lulled into the serendipitous frame of mind that only the talk of steelhead could induce was not only good medicine, it even made the most uncomfortable probing of certain orifices pass without any notice. One day when "the

Doc" was making his rounds through the Winston shop, as he often would, I inquired about his rumored brown trout buddies. His demeanor lit up. "You mean Floyd and Ethel?" I was in awe! Then, aglow with enthusiasm, he proceeded to give me blow-by-blow details about the encounters he had had with these two lunkers in two separate holes on the lower Beaverhead over the years. He was particularly fond of floating special friends to their lair and watching the reaction, as a well-directed cast would usually produce a commotion of colossal proportions somewhere near the friend's fly. But, he solemnly concluded, Floyd and Ethel were of a bygone era. The floods and subsequent droughts had changed everything, and nothing had been the same since.

Finding a big fish, at least for me, was no easy task. In fact, it became an obsession, and I never did locate a Floyd, an Ethel or a Spot. All of the fish I caught were never that big, not like the boatload of twenty-inchers I always seemed to hear about on a regular basis. If there were rumors of an unusually big fish hooked somewhere in the valley, I would sniff out the source and ferret through the details like an FBI agent looking for Jimmy Hoffa. I firmly believed that doing my homework would eventually result in the fish of my lifetime—and maybe, just maybe, grist for a story.

The unusually hot, sunny July that next year had become the standard for the drought-plagued period of the eighties. By the end of the month, the Big Hole would likely be begging for water from the irrigation ditches that would be diverting much of its flow. Although the fishing had been exceptional up to that point, it seemed tainted in light of the impending complications due to a lack of water. As the door slammed behind me when I entered the fly shop on a scorcher of an afternoon, Scott proclaimed his usual, "Kus! What's up?"

In return I barked my typical, "Not much." The Beatle's Sergeant Pepper provided the appropriate Lonely Heart's Club

accompaniment to my more-than-glum spirit. It was bad enough
my wife was working in California that summer, but hot weather
always puts me in a foul mood.

With the formalities concluded, Scott handed me a manuscript
and urged me to read it. It was something he had been working
on over the winter. *Fly Fisherman* wanted to publish another one
of his stories, but he needed to work out some of the kinks before
it ran. He especially wanted my approval for the couple of
paragraphs he wrote about me. Immediately transcending into
the oblivious outer reaches of our ozone-less atmosphere, I was
speechless and honored—fifteen minutes of fame (okay, maybe
two) in a Scott Waldie story. The wonders of it all! The makings
of a legend! "But...when you say I'm phlegmatic," I sheepishly
asked, referring to a descriptive passage in the text, "what does
that mean?"

Scott smiled, and said, "Look it up!"

I never did, though; I guess I was just too phlegmatic to care
about it anyway. As I continued, part of the plot centered around
his fabled big fish, Spot. Me, in a fishing story about a big fish! I
read along in ethereal bliss. The story developed nicely until Spot
ended up in a cooler at the hands of some lure-chucking
sportsman, and that event tied nicely into the subplot finale.

A knot of devastation twisted in my gut. Again I was
speechless, but for different reasons this time. My heart pounded,
my head ached, and my ears burned like they were just ripped
off by an errantly cast Yuk Bug. "You never told me that the
legendary Spot was reduced to fodder for the smoker! When did
this abomination occur?" I quizzed in a quivering voice. This
news hit me hard, because somewhere in the recesses of my
hidden desires, I had wished that Scott would take me to meet
Spot one day.

Scott's gaze was one of compassion, then he kind of chuckled.
"I write stories, not newspaper articles. Sometimes I rearrange
information for effect, and add a bit of fiction here and there

also, when it helps the story line. That's the beauty of it all. Heck, that's what writers do!"

"Meaning what?" I asked, impatiently waiting for him to get to the point.

"The last I knew, Spot still dwelled in that depression on the Big Hole," was his reply of both reprieve and relief. Although his last rendezvous was close to a year ago, Scott felt confident that the Great One, Spot, would still be at home. Then, get this! He offered to detail the exact whereabouts of this wondrous fish with the hopes that I, too, would get to know the brown trout of which dreams were made.

Christmas came early that year. Scott urged me to get over to the Big Hole as soon as possible, for the water was dropping quickly and it wouldn't be long before conditions would deteriorate beyond the realm of enticing even a ten-incher. Any aspiring writer would certainly recognize the opportunity in this offer. Proceeding to count the possibilities, "Spot Lives" or "The

Reincarnation of Spot" or "Spot, the Sequel" all ran through my head as probable theme selections for my first outdoor story.

I reached the precise location on the Big Hole early the next morning. It was a rather healthy walk from the nearest legal access, but I wouldn't have wanted it any different. The run was just how Scott had described it. In fact, his depiction was so accurate, it was as if it had been etched in the hard drive of my mind. First, I would have to cross two side channels. Then I would have to walk downriver until they both came together forming a deep pool where the main thrust of current carved an undercut along the opposite bank. As the run began to flatten out, there was a long length of inviting trout water. My eyes followed the flow, and the slightly protruding log beneath a row of willows that formed a quiet pocket was easy to locate. It was there the big fish dwelled.

That morning possessed all the characteristics that bring people to the Big Hole in the first place. Tea-colored water glowing with promise, active birds chirping songs of encouragement, the river was a picture-perfect scene of a trout angler's dream. Still cool in the shade, fingers of sunlight filtered through the rustling leaves of cottonwood. The zephyr morning breeze mixed sweet scents of sap with the warming pre-noon air—a portent of the heat that was sure to intensify later that afternoon. Cool, but not calm, I tied on a moderate-sized muddler and approached the "longed-for" depression, the home of Spot, with confidence. But I never did reach the *spot*.

Just then, a little movement on the bank caught my attention. Beyond the red, yellow, and black male western tanager, fleeing from its well-suited perch tucked safely on the riverside edge of a bushy willow, came an angler. But there was something very wrong with the image he projected, for only out of the pages of a Stephen King novel could anything have been more horrific. There, hanging from a rope, was the lifeless, partially dried-out form of a very big brown trout that stretched from well above the knee of this ghoulish creature down to the top of his boot. As if he couldn't wait to show off his prize, the angler held up the fish plainly for me to see. Puffed and proud, he announced, "Pretty nice, huh?" As the blood traced a trickle from the gill down the broad side of the once-beautiful male salmonid, the intruder's smile took on a grotesque twist at his cheek, which was distorted by the copious wad of a tobacco product—chunks of which still spotted the teeth displayed prominently from inside his wide-faced grin.

Although this fellow was likely a well-intentioned-somebody's-son, and not the ax murderer that he first appeared, I said nothing. Like a smoking gun, a discarded worm container on the bank told the story. If that was Spot, I didn't want to know. I didn't look for the scar; I could only speculate and hope that it wasn't there. The tear in my eye could have been from a speck of pollen. I wasn't sure. Before suffocating on the intensity of the moment, I got out of there—immediately!

On my way back to the vehicle, thoughts turned to Charlie Thomas. He used to keep big fish, lots of them, but that was just a part of the western culture way back when. At least, that's what I'd like to believe. In a former life I had kept my share of fish, too. And since it is not against the law to do so on many rivers, such judgement of those who do keep fish may be unfair. Undoubtedly, many anglers have gotten quite self-righteous about releasing fish these days, and for a lot of good reasons. For instance, there are just too many of us now. For another, it takes many years to grow a big fish. And with Spot in particular, he was kind of like a long-lost friend and a legend all rolled into one. Whether or not it was the Great One, probably the angler that morning would never have understood the distinction or appreciated the significance. It is a question of reverence, I suppose, for any fish to survive so long in any river. Killing and then eating it seems like such a waste, especially when it could be still alive fueling the hopes of the greater good.

Since then, the quest for big fish has lost all importance. Big fish are always best when they come as a surprise anyway, a rewarding prize for years of effort—much like the old man's fish in Scott's original piece. But just hooking a "trophy" once in a while keeps the storyteller in all of us alive and well.

I can't say I wasn't disappointed that morning on the Big Hole. Possibly, the literary scoop of a lifetime was just a cast away. But even if Spot were there that morning, he may have never taken my fly anyway. Fishing is all about hope, but sometimes despair wins out. Like *The Old Man and the Sea*, this big fish thing is an epic desire, a symbolic fantasy that haunts many anglers. And since big fish, like a mysterious, elusive force, will forever swim through the dreams of all who contemplate the inner being of any river, it might be said that a fish like Spot is the consummate metaphor of our very own souls. For some, it might further be said that catching Spot could have philosophical, if not spiritual, overtones. And who knows, for others a Spot encounter could bear Supreme implications as well.

As for me... A story! That's all I really wanted anyway.

At the River's Edge

Studiously watching every move, asking the appropriate questions along the way, he jotted notes from time to time on the tattered pad held in his hand. Before us stood the media icon I watched on television in my younger years, and all America befriended, as his "down home" *On the Road* journeys brought the lives of average folk throughout the country into the living rooms of Everyman. Charles Kuralt had recently retired from the public eye, but that obviously didn't mean retirement in the traditional sense. He was still at work writing another book about his favorite places around the country and, of course, the people who occupied these places. Since he had chosen southwestern Montana to build a restful retreat along the Big Hole River, this region topped the list. That particular day three of us were gluing wispy strips of bamboo under the watchful eye of his Yoda-like presence.

The Winston Rod Company was moved to Twin Bridges in 1974 from San Francisco by its former owners Tom Morgan and Glenn Brackett. This company of renown makes some of the finest fly rods on the international market, and with the interest in the sport rapidly growing since the showing of the movie *A*

River Runs Through It in 1992, Winston was firmly established to capitalize on the economic boom the movie provided the fly fishing industry. The company's "bread and butter" is the one hundred or so models of graphite rods it manufactures to suit almost any occasion of fly fishing opportunity—thousands are produced annually. On the other end of the spectrum, the one hundred or so individual bamboo rods constructed each year don't make or break the company, but rather connect it to a rod building tradition that goes back more than seventy years. Although the spirit of "past to present" is worth far more than the two thousand dollars each finely crafted bamboo fly rod commands, the inspiration provided to all admirers by the exquisite final product, even to those who do not fish, is priceless. Under a new generation of ownership since 1991, the company continues to move forward. A modern facility on the outskirts of town has positioned the business nicely to meet all challenges well into the next century. But in a little downtown back alley, the bamboo shop still remains firmly entrenched in the past, like a guiding beacon, constantly reminding the company and its employees of the roots from whence it came.

It was *this* spirit that Charles Kuralt was trying to capture in word. His inquiries were endless, and master rod builder Glenn Brackett, who continued on with the company after his interests were sold, provided this legendary figure with many answers about a complicated subject. Glenn has been at this trade for over twenty-five years now, placing him in an elite, but limited, group of bamboo experts with similar credentials. He has been sharing much of his knowledge with journeyman Jeff Walker whose talents equal the dedication he brings to the Winston bamboo tradition. Then there was me, a babe in the woods, learning the craft one slow step at a time.

Every Wednesday, the three of us gather in what is called a "cut and glue session," the only aspect of the process that requires a team effort. On a normal midweek get-together, the detailed process of binding glued strips (splines) of bamboo into tapered sections is a demanding effort made easier only by a constant philosophical dialogue amongst the three of us that even Plato would appreciate. We talk about such things as honor, intregrity, greed, overpopulation, the eroding standards of our fast-paced society, to mention a few topics, and although nothing is ever solved, we figure the final product may reflect these tiny bits of wisdom when the construction is completed.

For Charles (he insisted we didn't call him Mr. Kuralt), our weekly conclave was the perfect opportunity to gain knowledge into the fascinating, but complex, world of making a split bamboo or, as they say in the industry, cane rod. We certainly did not want to scare him away with our regular discussions; therefore, much of the day was devoted to a casual conversation that provided nonstop insights into the craft as well as our collective personality. Together we chatted like old friends. At one point, Charles kindly volunteered that he had one of my weekly nature articles clipped from the *Montana Standard* hanging on his cabin wall. He also shared, in jest, a career highlight when he was the featured topic of a David Letterman Top Ten List. "Cruising for babes with Walter Cronkite," he chuckled good-naturedly, and then continued in his characteristic drawl, "topped the ten things Letterman predicted I would do upon my retirement." He also talked about his life, and solemnly mentioned a recent trip to visit his aging father in North Carolina. It seemed he was grasping for a closeness that is often the elusive anomaly of a wandering spirit. By day's end, the four of us sat in a circle, trading stories and shucking peanut shells into the garbage can we surrounded. Charles even bought the beer. "Guess who came for peanuts today?" was the first thing I asked my wife upon returning home later that evening.

Since Charles had a way of making us ordinary folks seem special, later that night I reflected upon the sequence of events that led to this point in my life. Without a doubt, I too could relate to a life on the road. Embarking on a lifelong fishing journey during the early seventies was my attempt to make any sense at all out of the turmoil and strife that embroiled our country during that period. Consequently, the choice to make fishing my sole life pursuit was not a trivial decision, although it may be judged so by those with no frame of reference or ability to understand the impact that war has on every individual and every aspect of society. Fly fishing became the ultimate assertion of my escape from the conventional norms of the day as well as the vehicle used for the often overused, banal concept of "finding oneself." Inspired by the books of a few fishing greats, I learned one cast at a time. Exploring rivers—good ones, bad ones, mediocre ones—for the secrets they held became a monumental quest. Wandering the West in quiet solitude, the medium became the meaning. Jobs were predicated on their proximity to the stream, and everyone soon learned my unconventional priorities. Careful not to violate the devoutness of my pursuit, opportunities to guide professionally were avoided. For me, this fly fishing was a private thing—a blending of art, sport, religion, childhood, and oblivion. As with the noted angling judge and author Robert Traver, this was my small act of rebellion. He summed it up concisely, "...not that I regard fishing as being so terribly important but because I suspect that so many of the concerns of men are equally unimportant—and not nearly so much fun."

The decision to move to Twin Bridges was made impulsively one fall in the early eighties. This rather lifeless town that housed the unique fly rod manufacturer was known more for its trout than anything else, and even that was a best-kept secret. It was easy to understand why Glenn and Tom chose this sleepy corner of the world to relocate their rod building business. They made a product in which they each believed, and both avidly fished the product they made. A rare day would pass when one or the other wasn't off fishing somewhere. It was their intention that the sheer location of the Winston Rod Company would somehow assure that all the right elements would blend together into something special.

Small-town Montana evaluates and scrutinizes its new residents quite thoroughly, and if you pass the intangible test of trustworthiness, opportunity usually beats its way to your doorstep in the form of volunteer positions at the library or an invitation to join the Rotary Club. When Winston was looking to fill a position, this fortuitous opportunity came knocking one day as well. The chance offering to work for a noteworthy business in the fly fishing world developed into an ideal situation. Although there was the consideration of mixing business with pleasure, the making of Winston Rods was the perfect blend of craftsmanship, recreation, and meaningful expression. For years on end, every waking hour was devoted to either making a rod or fishing with one. The shop allowed the freedom to fish every hatch on any given river at the appropriate time and, while at home, every free moment was spent devotedly wrapping guides on as many rods as possible. I believed that love and passion for the avocation called fly fishing could be built into every rod, and that somehow it would make a difference. I also believed that an environment that could support trout can also lift the human spirit. For me, everything made sense at the river's edge.

Through the eclectic gathering of talented, offbeat individuals and the leadership of knowledgeable ownership, the company took on a life of its own. The energy of a common commitment to something that was much more than just a sport became the intangible bond that could not be measured in dollars and cents. When the opportunity to build bamboo rods came my way after many years of service, it was the evolutionary pinnacle of years dedicated to a singular cause.

In the world of fly fishing's creative spin-offs, perhaps the art of making a split bamboo fly rod is the most enthralling, even to the non-angler. Though this craft's tradition is relatively short-termed, only dating back to 1850s England, it was advanced by

American technology and know-how in the early 1900s. Hiram Leonard's use of Tonkin cane, which is still imported from China, in the development of the now standard six-sided hexagonal rod actually revolutionized rod making in the late 1800s. For over fifty years afterwards, names of craftsmen and companies associated with those names developed throughout the country, establishing a folklore presence that lives on for many of today's serious anglers. Young, Powell, Dickerson, Payne, Garrison and others are appreciated now more than ever by a growing contingent of bamboo aficionados as this modern day society whirls further away from the intricate commitment it takes to produce such a masterpiece. When one considers the comparatively crude technology these gentlemen had to draw from in their day, this thought inspires yet a greater appreciation for the many dimensions of their talents.

The Winston Rod Company contributed significantly to the world of bamboo as well. In fact, its hollow-fluted construction during the 1930s innovated the industry and subsequently influenced the way all rods were built. Unlike many other companies, Winston's bamboo tradition was able to survive the ascendancy of fiberglass as the primary new material used in the construction of fishing rods by the late 1940s. Its bamboo tradition has survived the many phases of the graphite revolution also. The revered contributions of Lew Stoner, Doug Merrick, and Gary Howells live on through the present-day guidance of Glenn and Jeff. To have an opportunity to sit at the feet of these Masters is truly an honor.

I learned quickly that the glamour of the job was overshadowed by the painstaking day-to-day, step-by-step process it took to transform a culm of bamboo into its magnificent final product. Like a cocoon evolving into a butterfly, the metamorphosis of bamboo does not take place overnight. Thousands of steps must be completed before each rod is able to expressively cast a fly. I also learned that the pursuit of perfection was like chasing a rainbow—a beautiful, but ever-elusive goal. From observing Glenn at work, I realized too that dealing with this medium was truly Zen in essence. In fact, the building of a bamboo rod draws one into a very special space while the consideration of Zen's many precepts fills the contemplative moments of the mind as the hands tend to the task. Although I never did quite hear "the sound of one hand clapping," I knew I must be making progress when the phrase actually started to make sense. The world of bamboo is a combined state of the mind, soul, and spirit, and the cane rod is the material manifestation of that world. The energy can be felt in each completed work as the symphonic crescendo of doing the right things for the right reasons.

"The best way to learn how to build a bamboo rod is to build one," according to Master Glenn. Having accomplished the rudiments of glass and graphite rod building through my previous years of experience was certainly an asset, so under Glenn and Jeff's guidance, I plunged headfirst into the wonderful opportunity I was offered. The bamboo process starts by selecting the appropriate poles (or culms). Unbelievably, raw bamboo is essentially a giant stalk of grass, about two to four inches in diameter and hollow down the center. Cut to five-foot sections, these lengths are split into workable strips, and then the nodes are sanded off each usable piece. At this point, these strips are milled into triangular rough cut strips and, subsequently, heat treated. A humidifier puts back into each individual piece a designated amount of moisture before each is passed through a series of tapered cuts on the milling machine, arriving at a final phase within an amazing .001-inch or less range of tolerance. After each is inspected and prepared, six splines are arranged with nodes staggered, glued, and bound tightly with string in one of our team sessions. Hung to cure for many months, it is now in the hands of the "bamboo Gods" to judge how perfectly the task has been performed to this point.

The Gods indeed smiled upon me, for after three months, I was blessed with several workable blanks from which my rod would be built. The process actually involved laying out two separate rods, but the one that captivated my interest most was the seven-foot three-inch rod that developed after careful inventory of my available blanks. Each piece must be cleaned, sanded, and then appropriately cut to size at the exact dimension on the blank to achieve the final desired taper and subsequent action. Once the tediously exacting process of fitting the duronz ferrules had been accomplished, the rod was ready for a cork handle. Before wrapping and varnish coating the thread, I chose to oil the exposed cane rather than varnish it. The actual Winston Rod would then be sprayed with a thin coat of varnish, providing a rich and lustrous finish.

Now all the rod needed was a seat built by the Winston expertise of Annette McLean and it was ready to field test. All in all, the process sounds easy enough... But to do all the exacting steps, it took thirteen months from start to finish. According to Glenn, bamboo rods aren't meant to be built on a timeclock. "In order to do something perfectly," he says, "a person has to be in a perfect frame of mind." I suppose, in my case, that happened within about thirteen months' worth of perfect moments. The rod casts like a sweet summer breeze.

I long believed that only the true masters of fly fishing deserved the privilege to fish cane. Besides, on a Montana-based budget, previously owning a decent bamboo rod was out of the question, and the opportunity to fish with one was as infrequent as finding true love at a singles bar. Like comparing skim milk to cream or polyester to silk, the melodic fluidity of cane's magical wandlike action defies description, especially for a dry fly enthusiast. For every ardent angler and connoisseur of the sport, eventually procuring a bamboo rod is a worthy goal. For me, the crowning achievement of my fly fishing ventures would now be to present a perfect cast with a not-so-perfect fly (my flies are always in need of skillful improvement) to a willing trout on a rod I was proud to have made.

The world of bamboo is a realm rife with wisdom, compelling one to strive for ideals deemed, I'm sure, too lofty by some and just pure foolhardy by others. When *Charles Kuralt's America* finally became available in the bookstore, there we were—Glenn, Jeff, and myself—making bamboo fly rods on the pages of the *September Chapter: Twin Bridges, Montana.* Since his visit, one of the finest museums in the country dedicated to the history of bamboo was opened in the new Winston facility located at the south entrance of town. Also, in the wake of the growing enthusiasm for fly fishing, the craft's allure has recently inspired a revolution of new age hobbyists and artisans dedicated to passing the ways of bamboo on to future generations.

In April, 1995, I was able to return to western New York's Oatka Creek. For me the whole trout concept came together on this gentle eastern stream in 1972. It was there, years ago, that I learned about the rhythms of the creek, its rising trout and its soothing water. Stepping back in time can be therapeutic. Nearly a quarter of a century had passed, and "the Oatka" had hardly changed at all. But I had. I was no longer on the run from the past. A journey of rivers helped me to resolve the darkness of that era. Time may not heal all wounds, but it sure does give everything a different perspective. There, in dreamlike silence, I caught a beautiful wild brown trout on the bamboo rod that symbolized the culmination of a long odyssey.

When word came of Charles's passing, I felt honored to be among the final "regular people" of the thousands with whom he had established a sort of brief, but I'm sure, significant connection over a notable existence. We never made that bamboo rod for him either. He kept postponing his order until he was certain about the specifications that would best suit his needs.

With great humility he made it very clear to us that his fly fishing abilities were not deserving of such an accouterment, but somehow we knew he was very worthy. Even now, we picture him casting that bamboo into the section of the Big Hole River that flows past his cabin. That water, it would seem, had the power to provide him an ever-fleeting glimpse of the home he had left behind for all those years "on the road" less traveled.

To all the rivers and all the trout, I owe much. Charles Kuralt's "day with the boys" made me realize just how lucky I have been. I will continue to build bamboo fly rods with my friends Glenn and Jeff, because it is a perfect way of life. And, above all, I will continue to follow the road that leads to water, because I believe—with all my heart—that everything really does make sense at the river's edge.

Tibby's Big Adventure

Picture a man and dog—say a black lab—silhouetted on a backdrop of a western river as the sun's final statement casts a pinkish hue over the mountains to the east. Add as well the descending shadows of evening, the soft breezes of twilight, and thousands of mayflies performing a ritualistic finale that completes their circle of life. While the dog sits obediently at the water's edge, the man lifts a limber fly line off the surface, and in the fluid rhythm of sequential backcasts, beadlets of river flick off into the grayness like diamond dust. One false cast, two, then three—the line wedges out perfectly and over the fly turns, fully extending to the end of a ten-foot leader, then delicately dropping on the darkening water—the fly inches toward a constantly vibrating ring. The man is hunched and watching as the rod tip is gently lifted—not jerked— with astute confidence. Then the rod bends emphatically, the ensuing battle unfolds, and the event is witnessed patiently by his best friend at a safe distance. Such idealism fills the dreams of most anglers. Stick a pipe in the fisherman's mouth, and a painting of the scene would be classic Americana.

When I go fishing, I hate to be bothered by any distractions, but there is something appealing about approaching the river with a canine companion. Why not? Cisco had Poncho, Batman had Robin; in fact, all great adventurers had their sidekicks, plain and simple. I really got the idea from a trip in early May a few years back when I met my friends from Twin Falls on the Green River. Dick and Delores fish more than any couple I know. And scheduling regular fishing jaunts together while juggling their respective private practices was no small feat. That effort alone was testimony to their devoted commitment to the sport they love. It was the rumor of 30,000 fish per mile, all rising in syncopated time to carpet hatches of *baetis parvis* as far as the eye could see, that brought us to Utah that week.

There were many locations where we could have gathered, but the three of us had our hearts set on pursuing surface feeders, and the reports from the Green were excellent. I am not a dry fly snob, but for my money, there is nothing that really compares to the thrill of the rise. Seasons of research have revealed that the serious western "dry flyer" can find willing surface feeders twelve months a year, but this requires a tremendous degree of flexibility, and even a greater degree of luck. While there is a good list of probable destinations in May that offer such opportunities, many of them, particularly in Montana, run the risk of low-level snowmelt fouling up the plans. And though tailwater fisheries are usually more dependable, calculated risks in the fishing sense still exist at this time of year. Reliable information indicated, however, that the Green was a good bet. It was there I met Gus.

Gus is Dick's vizsla, a sleek Hungarian hunting hound, and at the time he was a very young vizsla. Within minutes, it became obvious that this lean running machine was in serious need of some fine-tuning. Gus had a beam-me-up-Scotty quality about him; one second he was here, the next second he was barely visible about a half mile downriver. While I was enjoying the concept of harnessing this creature into man's best fishing buddy,

Dick was going nuts. Delores, locked into a no-nonsense fishing mode, was too busy looking for rising trout to be bothered. And though the frenetic Type-A approach to the world of trout is not uncommon these days, you can at least put a dog in a cage. It would be a while before Gus could ever settle into being the perfect fishing sidekick. Needless to say, Gus found himself relegated to the portable dog house for the week. When it comes to dry fly fishing, first things first.

Have you ever witnessed the effect that a four-foot rise in water within just a matter of hours has upon a fishery? The fish scoot about in a frenzy, and the angler gets very annoyed. As luck—bad luck—would have it, this was the very first week *ever* that an active attempt was made to save the Colorado squawfish from further population declines. The plan was to shoot massive doses of water down the river daily to assist the spawning process of this native species. And despite the immediate frustrations cast upon us persnickety fishermen, this attempt to save yet another threatened earth inhabitant was admirable. So, just about the time a small percentage of trout started to get loosened up for a day full of chasing our flies, along comes a three-foot torrent of water from the dam, scattering fish and anglers alike to safe lies and higher ground respectively. To make matters worse, the river would settle back down to a decent level a little before dark. Then, just as the fish began to rise to the surface once again, it *was* dark! Despite the good intentions on behalf of the squawfish, there were many unhappy anglers wandering the banks of the Green that week. But then came a glimmer of hope, a small morsel of reconciliation from the keepers of the dam. The day before my departure, the water normalized by mid afternoon, and the fish responded as if touched by some force of wreckless abandon. By evening we had shaken the blues caused by a week of resorting to various nymphing techniques. The three of us had finally landed several fish on floating blue-winged olive patterns in the afternoon and rusty spinners toward dark.

The next day, I knew I was in trouble early. I had already promised myself to be on the road by mid morning after the daily rise—water rise, that is. This would allow one-and-a half days to trek the five hundred miles back to southwestern Montana, and a booked commitment, through some serious snow country. Although it was May, snowstorms don't pay much attention to the calender in this part of the West. The day was gray and, by all weather reports, it looked as if I would need every last minute to make the trip. As the fish started to rise on schedule that morning, the hours clicked by quickly in anticipation of the daily slug of water; but it never happened. That day Dick, Delores, and I *caught* a glimpse of why we came to Utah; maybe there were 30,000 fish per mile, but we were too busy to count. Lulled into hypnotic bliss, it was dark before I could analyze my plight. It happens all the time. "Just one more cast," I tell myself; but even with the best of intentions, I can never quit. I had kind of a squeamish feeling pulling out of the campground at five o'clock in the pouring rain. Even Gus couldn't figure the wisdom of that move.

The good news was that the steady rain only flirted with changing to snow after reaching Pinedale. *If I could only make it to Jackson Hole for the evening*, I thought, again deluding myself. My mind pondered the "dog as man's best friend" notion for a good portion of the journey. I had traveled for years with a seasoned cat, but the thought of a cat sitting streamside just doesn't inspire that alluring sense of field and stream. Then it struck me. *Wait a minute*, I thought, *I do have a dog at home*. Well, it's kind of a dog. Actually my...*gulp*...our dog heavily prefers my wife's company, and you really get the distinct feeling that Tibby would be insulted to be called a dog. You know the type—a fuzzy, furry Lhasa apso that spends much of her life planted on a plush recliner watching TV, surrounded by an assortment of dog bones, Liv-A-Snaps, and dried up pancakes. In fact, she'd walk a mile for a pancake! Tibby is kind of like a lawn ornament for the living room; but just maybe with a little work...hmm. It was well after midnight when I rolled into a campground on the outskirts of Jackson Hole. The rain was really coming down.

I awoke to the sound of Niagara Falls falling on my camper, but at least it wasn't snow. The day's task, however, would be a tough one—getting over Teton Pass. As far as mountain passes go, this is a ten. It doesn't mess around with nifty switchbacks that slowly wind the traveler to the summit one step at a time. This one goes straight up a big mountain, and then straight down again. And it *never* not snows there, even in July, at least whenever I try to go over it in July. There was no question, getting over the pass would take strategic planning. And where best to set up command central but the Mickey D's that sits on Jackson's main drag, just across from the intersection that leads to the sky. From this ideal location, I could get a cholesterol McBiscuit, endless coffee, and watch for some sort of sign. About two bites into breakfast, a big orange snowplow with lights a-blinking and tons of sand turned onto the highway. Slowly, it started up the hill. Things were looking up! By the time the sandwich and the appropriate amount of coffee had been consumed, the plow would have dealt with most of the white hazard on the highway and sprinkled it with a generous application of its load.

The rain had changed to snow about halfway up the hill, and when I finally caught up with the plow, it was about one mile below the summit. In fact, after passing a '75 Ford pickup fishtailing through the sand, my Nissan was confidently chugging up the hill directly behind the orange monster like Barry Sanders following his blocker to the goal line. Since the surface was at that in-between stage, simultaneously freezing and melting, the road was still very slick. About one half mile below the apex, the grade steepens. The heavy, wet snow was substantial at this point, and the snowplow's progress became slower and slower and slower...until it stopped. Then it was kind of like a nightmare, maybe worse, when the truck's course changed direction. It started to freely slide back toward the Nissan like a twenty-ton sled. There was panic emanating from the state truck—brake lights frantically blinking, a sand dune flying from its payload as the beastly machine slowly twisted sideways. The traffic behind had put me in a squeeze. So there I sat, griping the steering wheel so tight that white knuckles were about to rip through my skin.

At times like these, you have to blame something. That's the American way. I started cursing that damn river. If only it had risen on schedule, I would have avoided this whole mess. The mind gets ethereal, too. I wondered if there were any trout rivers in heaven, or dogs for that matter, assuming the most optimistic scenario. Then, about three feet from my diminutive pickup, the orange gargoyle came to a halt. Have you ever noticed, there's always one idiot in every crowd? At that moment, a SUV from behind got just enough traction to work itself into the passing lane before gridlocking on the semi-melting surface, blocking it totally, and there it stayed in suspended animation. The situation was not good; freefalling back to Jackson loomed as a distinct possibility. And then there was the traffic coming from the other side of the pass. It had to go somewhere! Taking to the highway shoulders, the vehicles blew by those of us stranded on this slanted ice rink like so much space junk traveling at warp speed. It was then I made some idle entreaties which included deals like joining a Buddhist monastery, enlisting with Mother Theresa, giving up fishing forever. Anything! *Please!*

It may be hard to believe, kind of like a miracle, but about that time the sun broke through the clouds. Then those rays of light reached right out of the sky, touched the highway, and pushed the already near-melting surface over the freezing point. Five minutes later, we all drove away in slush, through the eight inches of unplowed snow and over the pass. That left me wondering. Am I legally obliged to follow through on any of those aforementioned promises? The state worker was still chaining up the truck tires as the Nissan was gathering momentum.

The weather break was extremely short-lived. Heavy snows throughout the Island Park region of Idaho changed to blizzard conditions after passing over Raynold's Pass into Montana. When it comes to the Treasure State, springtime in the Rockies sometimes translates into endless winter. Fishing trips were supposed to be relaxing—but no more for a while, I vowed, after this Dante-ish journey. Inch by inch, through sideward-driving snow, the expedition progressed, and finally, the friendly confines of Twin Bridges came into full view. It was early May and barely twenty degrees. Get real!

My wife, Debra, asked how the trip went. "Fished in a flood, drove through a blizzard, nearly crushed by a snowplow," I replied. But my rantings were patently dismissed as typical fisherman fantasy. "Did you catch any fish?" She chortled. I had barely answered when she anxiously changed the subject. She then informed me that she had accepted the summer teaching position we had already discussed in April. For the whole month of June, she would be in Tennessee. It sounded like a great opportunity—especially for me. I knew that meant Tibby would be my responsibility. I turned to the white lump of fur on the chair, smiled, and asked, "Want to go fishing, girl?"

Since promises made under duress don't count (just ask any lawyer), I didn't join a monastery or give up fishing. As for that silly vow, no more trips actually meant just for a few weeks. Since June was barely around the corner, preparations had to be made for the upcoming trip with my...*gulp*...dog.

The period from the end of May into early June was a very wet one. As the rain and snow continued, I knew most of Montana's waters would be unfishable. In normal years, melting snow combined with any precipitation at all fills many western rivers to overflowing with off-colored, cold runoff, leaving a limited list of fishing options. This usually happens during June. Undaunted by the challenge, I had a series of backup plans. The first was a weekend trip to Henry's Fork designed to work out some of the kinks that may arise from traveling with my newly considered fishing companion.

Actually, Tibby had been a part of the family for several years, but most fishing trips were planned around *not* taking her anywhere. She hates putting her four feet into a vehicle. Granted, this was not a good trait for a fishing dog. On trips Tibby did make, Debra was always along to tend to her needs. Since Henry's Fork is a tailwater, conditions should have been just right despite the high water everywhere else— and there was always something hatching there. To make this a rather easy outing, we headed over Saturday afternoon to prepare for a full day of fishing on Sunday.

Despite a minor anxiety attack on the way, Tibby survived. She only threw up once. Man and dog then spent the evening camping and, without incident, arrived at the newly paved parking lot on the outskirts of town early the next morning. Although the State Park section of the Fork that flows through Harriman Ranch does not allow dogs, this piece of water was still closed for another week. I had planned to fish the easily accessible Last Chance section of the river anyway, apparently along with several others. As the lot began to fill, I began to feel a bit uneasy. But before my disappointment got overbearing, I noticed several of the patrons were accompanied by their "best friends" as well. It was beautiful—a convention of fishing buddies. There were some fine specimens too, mostly black and golden labs answering to names like Rex, Thor, Caesar, Satan, etc. With a snap of a finger, these dogs would sit; a call of their names and all barking would cease.

Sitting on my tailgate, the ritualistic suiting up for the day began. The parking lot was buzzing with activity. About the time my one leg got sucked up into its neoprene sheath, Tibby decided to pull out of her leash for an unscheduled walk while Rex, Thor, et al. voiced their disapproval rather forcefully. I snapped my fingers, but that didn't work. I then clapped my hands, and yelled loudly, "Tibby, stay!" But she kept walking. "Tibby, sit!" But she kept walking. Hopping through the parking lot was awkward with only one unrestrained leg. "Tibby, come back here...pleeease!" But she seemed to have a mission as she aimed at the trailer parked on the other side of the paved expanse like a heat-seeking missile. By the time I hobbled over, the dog was scratching on the camper door. A fellow peered out the window and laughingly queried, "Who's walking whom?" I assumed he was Ed, because of the two letter name written on the door. He confirmed that he was.

"My...*gulp*...my wife's dog doesn't pay much attention to me," I replied with an apologetic tone. "I don't suppose you are cooking pancakes?" Ed stared at me like I was the all-knowing Amazing Kreskin, then he acknowledged incredulously that he was. Tibby's nose rivaled any dog's in the parking lot.

Ed looked exactly like you'd picture a guy whose name "Ed" was roughly scrawled on his door in black paint. His white T-shirt, bulging belly, slicked-back but thinning gray hair, and dangling cigarette gave him away immediately. We conversed a while through the screen. Ed brought me up to date on the happenings of "the Fork" since opening day. The river's rainbow populations were still very much depressed from the water mismanagement of the eighties. The potato farmers, not the fish, were the most important element in this equation. It seems most harm occurred during the winter months when flows were cut back drastically and ice would collapse upon the small trout taking refuge at the river's edge. He confirmed that, despite a plenitude of PMDs and Baetis, there were very few rainbows to be found, but those few were rather big. On the other hand, Ed confided, he never comes to Henry's Fork for trout anyway. Here we go, I figured, some kind of nut! Ed continued that he prefers to search the flat spring creek-like water for the unusually large whitefish that the river supports, and most people ignore. Whoa! At that point, I was ready to pick up the dog and run really fast back to my pickup!

"You ought to try it," he urged with all the confidence of a leading authority in the art of catching whitefish on a dry fly, "the big ones usually feed by themselves, and they fight real good."

He added that his refined studies revealed whitefish, when surface feeding, leave a bubble on the water commensurate to their size. He uses this precise information to locate *big* whitefish, and to prevent the annoying mistake (at least in Ed's mind) of hooking "one of them there rainbows." Obviously, Ed had slipped into a Sunday morning, pulpit-preaching frame of mind, looking to convert the masses, one lonely soul at a time, to follow the Great Whitefish to the throne of salvation. Scratching my head as I put my other leg in the waders, I wandered back to my rig. Dog in arms and baffled by Ed, I could only lament the stifled opportunities flowing before me that day thanks to Idaho's potato lobby.

Dogs, I found, do cut into an angler's mobility. Maybe that's why Rex, Thor, et al. and their masters spent much of the day around and about the parking lot perfecting one hundred-foot double hauls. Fueled by these shattered images, Tibby and I patrolled the shoreline for any likely prospects. After about an hour, I spotted a nose ever so slightly poking up by a clump of dislodged weeds about thirty feet from shore. I placed Tibby under the sparse shade of a dwarfed willow and explained my strategy. But before I could finish, she was asleep.

Rising once every five minutes or so, hardly noticeable, this extremely finicky creature snubbed my offerings for close to two hours. I could tell, though, it was big. Since I usually resist all temptations to seduce any halfhearted riser with a subsurface emerger pattern, I locked myself into the parameters of taking this fish cleanly off the surface. Snobbery, maybe, but it all depends upon how you define your own challenges; therein lies the individual subjectivity of the sport. In the sunshine on that particular morning, the hatches were scant, so I finally went back to the standard #18 parachute Adams. My twenty-foot upstream casts were automatic by that point, and it was almost time for this fine fish to make another rise to the surface, so I readied myself. Perseverance finally paid off, for on about the tenth cast with the sure-fire Adams, the fish barely sipped the fly off the surface, and then the fight was on. It was dogged combat (excuse the pun), but not like some of the battles of past years when these screamers would use the great width of the river to their advantage. I subsequently wrestled with the quarry for several minutes as it tangled in and around the weeds. Finally, the twenty-plus inch fish was landed. It was a beaut! And I'd like to leave the story at that (for the rest of the tale is rather distasteful, and I really hate to get into it.) Somehow, during the fight, the alleged trout had transformed itself into a whitefish! To tell the truth, I wasn't looking for bubbles; but thinking back, I did recall seeing a few as big as golf balls.

I should have still been excited, I suppose. Years ago, "whities" were just tossed into the fields adjacent to many western rivers as a symbol of a fisherman's disgust. I always thought that to be a very sad statement on behalf of sportsmen, and it just may be the same residual attitude that continues to haunt the whitefish today. Anglers shouldn't scorn whitefish, but they do. At the moment I released the trophy, I thought I heard a snicker from over my shoulder. But when I turned, Tibby was still asleep (I think).

How come you never lose a whitefish? That's one of those great all-time metaphysical questions like "how many angels can fit on the head of a pin." Some fish are best lost, for basking in the glory of what might have been is what really makes most of us fishermen masters of our own illusions anyway. Of course, the first person I bumped into on the way back to the tailgate casting clinic was Ed, garbed and ready for action. I hated to tell him, but I did. By the way he reacted to the report, you'd have thought he'd just seen Elvis walking through the parking area. He all but knelt at my feet as if to pay homage to the King of the Great Whitefish's Second Coming. He grilled me for thirty minutes on the details of this monumental display of piscatorial prowess. Just then Tibby finally paid big dividends; as she tugged at her leash, I kindly excused myself and told him we had to get going or she'd probably take a big dump right where we stood. There's only so much whitefish talk a man, or dog, can handle.

We (man and dog) fished until dark and finally made several casts to a late-evening rainbow with no success. But the day wasn't a complete loss; since I avoided every subsequent bubble, I never caught another whitefish, either.

About the only thing anyone needs to know about a Lhasa apso is that it is a smallish dog with a lot of long, thick hair. When standing, it is hard to tell the front parts from the back parts until it starts to move, and even then it's hard to know whether it is walking forward or backward. Bred as a Tibetan indoor palace guard dog, you could say an appreciation of the good ole outdoors isn't exactly in its genes. But Tibby's first attempt at becoming a fishing dog was not only a noble effort, she was a good sport about it, too. The next journey would be a true test of her fortitude.

As the precipitation continued to fall in its many forms, the western rivers continued to rise. Apart from tailwater opportunities that were likewise reaching stages of unfishabilty, the choices for our next venture were severely limited. Unless...? Out of the past, a northern Idaho river emerged from memory, and it held some possibilities. Flowing from low-level mountains that dealt with spring runoff at least a month earlier than the rest of the northern Rockies, the Coeur d'Alene River, which has withstood the pressures of logging much longer than it should have, had the reputation of running clear early in the season. There was an added attraction, as well. When the June water supply is ample, there is the potential of encountering a rather large strain of adfluvial westslope cutthroat dwelling in the deeper runs and holes; this possibility was especially enticing. After the spring spawning session in the river, these fish drop back to the large lake of the same name to spend the summer. This return trip depends greatly upon conditions, for as the water drops, the fish retreat. It is the lucky angler who ends up in the right place at the right time on the Coeur d'Alene. And with all that rain, the river might just be right.

There was nothing to lose. All other possibilities were moot, except for a return to Henry's Fork, but the memory of one twenty-inch whitefish was more than I could stand for this season. A few phone calls revealed no up-to-date info on the Coeur d'Alene's condition, so I informed the dog we'd take a three hundred-mile drive to check things out. I don't claim to be a mind reader, but when Tibby crawled under the sofa as I packed the truck, I got a good idea how she felt about the plan. Bribing her with pancakes, I promised there would be more where those came from when we got to our destination.

The Jefferson, Clark Fork, Blackfoot, and Bitterroot Rivers were all variable shades of brown on the afternoon the journey began. Although Rock Creek holds on longer than most other western Montana waters, even it was high and turning colors. The upper sections would still have salmon flies, but in the continuing rain, those prospects didn't seem too appealing. Upon reaching the summit of Lookout Pass, I realized the chances of finding fishable water in Idaho faded in the dim grayness of late afternoon as the accumulation of wet snow on Interstate 90's surface formed a treacherous layer of slush. When we arrived at the Coeur d'Alene, there was no one at any campground. In the dreary black gloom of evening, we tried to find the perfect place to set up. The steady downpour accentuated the smell of cedar wafting through the campsite, as well as the sinking feeling in my gut that I should have crawled under the sofa with the dog that morning instead of quixotically tilting at unfishable rivers. The dismayed look upon Tibby's face reflected her displeasure. "Wanna pancake, girl?" I asked.

The moisture at daylight came in the form of a heavy drizzle. The density of the morning air dripping off the Douglas firs that encompassed the surroundings scented the camper, and these earthly smells went beyond the nose. They penetrated the olfactory memory bank, triggering a flood of memories from years past. Looking out at our choice of camping locations made in total darkness, I said to my loyal travel mate, "Tibs, we did good!" Although the river was out of sight, the flush of water echoing off the adjacent slopes of the opposite shore filled my heart with anticipation. It was time to take a look.

The river was running full, but it still possessed the distinct characteristics of a run, a riffle, and a pool. More importantly, the water was totally and wonderfully clear. Realizing now that the series of pools in the catch-and-release area of the upper river would be in prime shape, I took Tibby on an exhilarating walk full of unbridled enthusiasm. I found that a dog provides a good object at which to direct idle conversation; in other words, a socially acceptable way to talk to yourself. Detailing the plans for the day out loud, I informed my companion there was no real need to get on the river before mid morning. After I checked the water again with guarded optimism, the sun briefly poked through the low-hanging clouds, offering even more confidence in what appeared to be one of the few approachable rivers within a five-hundred-mile radius of Twin Bridges.

By afternoon, a handful of westslopes had been fooled by various offerings matching a hodgepodge mix of naturals from pale morning duns to various stoneflies; but several other fish demonstrated the obvious discretion that comes from seeing far too many imitations. Who said cutthroat are dumb! All trout caught so far were resident river or fluvial fish; there was no sign of the bigger versions. Tibby accepted her role as river dog, sleeping in a hole she dug for herself next to a log. She even acted interested in the activity at one point, observing from a well-positioned perch, until one of my backcasts came forward minus the fly. A quick check revealed a startled Lhasa looking a bit like Chicken Little, but with a rather large sofa pillow stonefly imitation stuck in the thick hair on the top of her head. After that, she crawled back into the hole.

All went well until the afternoon thunderstorm started dancing lightning across the mountaintops. The cracking thunder resounded like a cannon, the rain came down in buckets, the dog was hysterical, and the fish were rising like they had never seen a downpour before. Using the just-one-more-cast method, I finally hooked a fine cutthroat that had the deep, thick appearance of lake-run fish—no question about it. Looking at the huddled quivering ball of wet fur, and alerted to the imminent danger as lightning flashed at the same instant thunder exploded, I started to bolt back to the vehicle—but the dog was too catatonic to respond. It was a long, wet walk back to the vehicle with dog in one arm, rod in the other, and electricity sizzling through the waterlogged atmosphere.

The next morning we stayed close to camp. Neither of us was thoroughly dry from the soaking experience of the night before, but the morning sunshine breaking through the fog speeded up the drying process while cutting through the accumulated discomfort that accompanies bone-chilling dampness. By early afternoon, another few fish were released, including a very nice adfluvial female. The sky was blue and the afternoon warm. I looked at Tibby and remarked that it would be a fine day for exploring new water.

After finding a little-used pulloff to park the truck, we entered the woods several miles upstream where the river bends out of sight from the highway. Tibby enjoyed this part of the venture until the trail started to show signs of disappearance. A twist here, a turn there—I encouraged my loyal fishing buddy to bear

with me; the river had to be over there, somewhere. The heat
created the ironic-sweat-dripping humidity of a Brazilian rain
forest as we plodded in the general direction of the water. Cutting
through the moose bog was probably a bad idea, but turning
back wasn't even an option. Rod in one hand, dog in the other,
and knee-deep in primordial ooze, I trudged along. Thoughts of
Humphrey Bogart's *African Queen* flooded my head in the insanity
of the moment. Crawling over fallen logs became a monumental
gauntlet of exhaustion. Precariously balancing the dog on each
toppled tree, I struggled out of the muck, over the downfall and
back into the muck, and then continued to the next one. I could
tell that this "fishing buddy" business was wearing thin on Tibby.
When, after crossing the slough, the gentle sounds of a soothing
flow of water broke through the dense thickets and gnarled brush
still remaining, our spirits were revitalized. Finally, as we broke
through, I just stood and looked in disbelief. Like a page out of a
Kafka novel, the futility of this harrowing jaunt was confirmed
when Tibby walked over to the hole she had dug next to the log
the day before, crawled in and just laid down. It was the same
pool we had been blown off the night before, a mere five-minute
walk from another access point on the highway.

By the time we exited the forest, however, the bluebird sky
had transformed into a mass of extremely dark thunderheads. I
never made a cast. The lightning began to dance across the
mountaintops, cracking thunder resounded like a cannon, the
rain came down in buckets, the dog was hysterical once again,
and the fish were rising like they had never seen a downpour
before. This *deja vu* of absurdity continued. Looking at the huddled
quivering ball of wet fur, and alerted to the imminent danger as
lightning flashed at the same instant thunder exploded, I started
to bolt back to the vehicle—but the dog was too catatonic to
respond. You know the rest, and probably have even concluded
by now, that the pickup was parked a good mile-and-a-half further
up the road.

The rain continued throughout the night and into the following day. I had breached every last ounce of trust I'd built with my fishing companion. There weren't enough pancakes in the world to continue to bribe her. The weary look on Tibby's face said it all. I've always liked the rain, but after six weeks of battling snowstorms and blizzards, thunderstorms and deluges, even I had grown weary of the elements. By noon, the rain was coming down even harder, and the thought of climbing into wet gear had about as much appeal as eating a raw egg. I turned to my loyal companion and said, "Let's go home."

We were parked overlooking a very nice stretch of the Coeur d'Alene. Rain has a mesmerizing effect as it pummels the surface of a river. The normal crystal-clear water can take on an opaque appearance as the millions of raindrop-created mini-ripples cause the flat light to refract or diffuse off the surface in a blurred sort of way. While I was daydreaming about the physics responsible for this phenomenon, a beautiful cutthroat rose to take something off the surface. In the flatness of the milky-looking water, the fish stood out as clearly as a large photograph. Details were strikingly observable. Then another rose, and then another. Immediately I hopped out of the truck and slipped down the hill to the riverside; I had to discover the *biology* responsible for this phenomenon. And there, quietly riding the gentle currents, was the granddaddy of all mayfly hatches—hundreds upon hundreds of *emphemerella grandis*, the large western green drake.

Opportunities to fish the green drake hatch come along infrequently enough to realize a good thing when it was happening. I knew what I had to do, but try explaining that to a travel-weary dog who expected to be on the road that afternoon. I put a big fluffy blanket on the passenger seat and placed her on it. Then I stacked the remaining dogbones, Liv-A-Snaps, and pancakes next to her—all the comforts of home, with just the television lacking. "You can watch the action from the window, Tibs." I promised her we'd be on the road that evening.

The anticipation of the moment eradicated all discomfort associated with suiting up in wet paraphernalia and heading down to stream side in the pouring rain. Keeping a fly floating in this present round of extreme wetness would be a challenge, but the imitation *grandis* I would be using was bushy, and it held a generous portion of floatant. Fish—big ones—started to rise at various locations within the large, long pool. Like magic, the motherlode of adfluvials materialized to slurp in abundant amounts of green drake duns while topping them off with a baetis dessert. Within the next few hours I landed the nicest westslope cutthroats I have ever seen. The chill became almost unbearable, but the uniqueness of the situation spurred my relentless desire to see this hatch to its completion.

There was one enticing fish that kept rising very infrequently from a nondescript shallow riffle, and there were absolutely no bubbles. Twice the fish came up to my imitations. Seductively, it refused my offerings both times. Making a mental note as to the position of this teaser, I fished other sections of the pool while watching for that big adfluvial to make one more move. By late afternoon, the rain had ceased, and the sun made an indolent effort to sneak through the dismal sky. The hatch was over. I was forty feet below the exact spot when the big cutthroat rose again, possibly for the last time.

I lifted my limber fly line off the surface, and in the fluid rhythm of sequential backcasts, beadlets of river flicked off like diamond dust. One false cast, two, then three... The line wedged out perfectly, over it went, fully extending to the end of a ten-foot leader. The fly dropped on the darkening surface a few feet in front of the fish. Ever so slowly the offering inched its way to the exact spot. Hunching, watching, I confidently lifted the rod tip at the precise time the fish intercepted the fly. The rod bent emphatically and then the fight. In the end, the finest male westslope cutthroat I may ever see lay on its side in the shallow water at my feet. The post spawning colors were stunning, and its elongated trunk made the ten-inch spotless section in the middle of its long greenish-tan body pronounced. The only thing missing from the moment was Tibby, attentively looking from her vantage point. But when I glanced up toward the parked Nissan, she wasn't there. It would have made a lousy painting anyway, and I don't smoke a pipe.

When I got back to the truck, Tibby was sleeping on her blanket, still surrounded by bribed goods. She didn't stir when I recounted the events of the afternoon. I told her she should have been there. Then I patted her on the head, thinking out loud once again, "That's *my* dog!"

For some, fishing is entirely an individual event. I informed her that she had been a faithful companion, but from now on I'd have to go it alone. "You know how it is, kid. Adventurers can't be tied down. We need our space. It's a big world out there."

The sun, which by then had completely broken through the dissipated evening clouds, was just disappearing behind the western mountains as we pulled away from the Coeur d'Alene.

Driving off into the sunset, I thought I heard a sigh come from Tibby's seat.

In fact, I know I did.

The Border of Reality

    I always break into a cold sweat while waiting in line at the border to either get into Canada or to get out of it. Our family often vacationed in Ontario when I was a child, and my father always put the fear of border guards into his two children as we approached the crossing booths. According to him, they were more powerful than God. Then he always warned us to not say anything stupid or else we'd likely go to jail. Those apprehensions must have stayed with me ever since because, to tell the truth, I can never guarantee I won't say something stupid.

    But some fears may be well founded. There was the time that I attempted to cross in the early seventies with a distant friend who was known to toke a joint now and then (of course, he actually inhaled as well). I was in desperate need of a ride from Detroit to Buffalo, so this friend contrived a reason to take me and off we went. Since we were taking the shortcut across Ontario, I made him swear that he had no drugs in his possession before I climbed into his Datsun 240Z. He crossed his heart. Instinctively, I should have realized such a vehicle would raise a red flag alert at the border. Needless to say, three customs officers spent a good part of the morning combing through his sportscar. During the entire search, I stood there like a dummy, picturing twenty years of hard time breaking rocks in a local quarry. But after two hours, to my relief, the officials signaled that we could be on our way. When we got back into the vehicle there were about two-hundred pot seeds stacked in neat rows on his dashboard.

So there I was again, this time in remote Minnesota, waiting at the border for the custom officer to extend the obligatory permission to enter Canada. The line was long. They like to make you wait so you can reflect upon all the horror stories you may have heard about crossing the border over the years. So I passed the time thinking about the tale a friend once related about his sister and a less-than-intimate boyfriend as they attempted the same feat in New York. It made me chuckle. His sister's friend was a modern hillbilly from the backwoods of Arkansas, and this was to be his first adventure into a foreign country. "If the guy at customs asks you if you have anything to declare," the sister jestfully instructed her naive companion, "just tell him that you declare Canada is a beautiful country." She then added the afterthought, "These guys love to be flattered." The subsequent interrogation went well until the border guard asked, "Do you have anything to declare?" In his best Jed Clampett twang the young man assertively pronounced, "I *do declare*, you sure *do* have a beautiful country." Naturally, the rest of the night was spent trying to explain that he wasn't actually a refugee from the land that inspired the movie *Deliverance*.

As I drove into the booth, the official took a different tact this time. "State your citizenship." His stern words blurted through my window like a belch from a baloney sandwich.

"USA," was my casual reply.

"Your purpose for entering Canada?"

"Going fishing. For steelhead on Lake Superior's north shore." Again, the reply was short and casual.

"Are you bringing any tobacco, firearms or alcohol into Canada?"

"No."

He stared at me and the goofy-looking Lhasa apso sitting next to me. "C'mon. Every fisherman brings alcohol along with them when they enter Canada."

A brief but uneasy pause ensued. Sweat began to form on my brow.

"Maybe they do. But I'd rather not drink alone." A short but sensible response—I thought. In fact, I'm quite sure it didn't sound too stupid.

A few minutes later, however, my truck was being ransacked by a young guard at a distant point where Minnesota ends and Canada begins. So who's laughing now? I figured 1996 was not a good year to enter Canada if you were from Montana anyway. The Unabomber, on the one hand, and the FBI standoff in rural Jordan, Montana, with that crackpot, gun-toting group of radicals on the other, cast suspicious doubts upon the rest of us scrupulous residents of the Big Sky State. Guilt by association, I would imagine. Preparing for that eventuality, I took particular care to trim my beard and cut my hair before leaving Montana with the hopes that I would bear no resemblance whatsoever to Ted Kazcynski. As it turned out, I had then transformed myself into the image and likeness of one of those screwball militia personalities. This particular group of social misfits called themselves Freeman. As the search continued, my mind drifted.

The trip to this point had already been a bust from a fishing standpoint. The past winter was one of the worst on record for the entire area, and it had lasted well into spring. When I arrived in Duluth a few days earlier, the city seemed to emanate a collective gloom only Prozac could cure. The endless oppression of nasty weather was reflected in the faces of the residents as they desperately waited for a break—kind of like Rover awaiting table scraps. While getting out of the truck to take a timely coffee break at the local Mickey D's—*whoosh!*—the forty mile per hour northeast wind took my hat for a ride through the parking lot. Bundling up against the gale in a wool Maine hunting jacket, I made my way to the front door. It was May twenty-second.

"Here's your coffee," the rather elderly counter lady announced with a scowl that could leave a person breathless. Given another place or time she could have passed for anybody's grandmother, but looking into her face as well as those of the other crew members, I had apparently entered the land of the McZombies. Since the grumpy edge that accented her robotic activities did not invite further comment on my part, there was no way I'd dare ask for cream. "That'll be ten cents," she barked, "senior discount included."

Looking around to make sure she was addressing me, and seeing no else one there, I then found myself feebly fumbling for my wallet and ID to provide solid evidence that I was still only forty-nine, years away from officially becoming a senior! Maybe she forgot her glasses. Sure, there are a few gray hairs here and there, but three days on the road shouldn't have aged me *that* much. Only some sort of time warp could explain the confusion. It wasn't so long ago I was actually trying to assert that I was *old enough*, but now attempting to verify I was "under age" proved particularly hard on the ego. The counter lady was taking another order when I came to my senses. Hmm, ten cents! What the heck, I thought. I was going to like this senior citizen stuff.

Taking a place alone in the corner next to a table full of *fellow* seniors, I couldn't help overhearing their conversation. By then I figured the characteristic scowl was a genetic mutation, possibly an environmental adaptation passed on to generations of Minnesotans living in the area. "It's really not bad out there today," one bold soul announced to the table. A quick check outside indicated nothing had changed within the past five minutes. The flag at the bank was still about ready to rip off the pole. Then my furtive glance toward the table revealed no smiles on the faces of the woeful-looking group. In fact, there was no reaction whatsoever to this witless proclamation except for a unified nod of agreement. At this point, I intuitively sensed that this fishing trip was doomed.

Later that day, the folks at Minnesota's Department of Natural Resources confirmed my fears. Although I had arrived in the area at what would normally be considered the perfect time frame, the long winter and late spring had left most of the state's rivers entering Lake Superior in varying stages of unfishability. Additionally, recent downpours and snowmelt filled them to the brim. Unfortunately, I had come to fish for the elusive Minnesota steelhead that should be entering the tributaries during this period. This is a tough run to intercept even under ordinary conditions, so the prospects were as hopeless as they seemed.

Researching the steelhead of the Great Lakes has become a personal passion. Most people do not realize that these magnificent fish were introduced into various areas of all five massive fresh-water lakes during the late 1800s. In fact, naturalized populations of these migrating rainbows have existed in the Great Lakes longer than the ever-popular brown trout have lived in Montana. Although the steelhead numbers are heavily supplemented by hatcheries in many locations, the importance of the Great Lakes' wild steelhead has gained much recognition over recent years, and figure prominently in future management plans throughout the entire system.

Minnesota's tributaries are unique. Most of the high-gradient streams entering into Superior have a natural barrier in the form of a falls within close proximity to the lake. There are only one hundred eighty miles of water that are able to be utilized by steelhead in this state, and several of those miles occur on the Knife River where the barrier was artificially altered for fish passage. Despite these facts, small but significant wild runs were established in many of Minnesota's tributaries throughout most of the twentieth century. By the 1980s, many of the runs had dwindled considerably, leading to drastic present-day changes in

regulations and management. Although studies are being conducted to determine exact reasons for the decline, factors may be too complex to pinpoint. Since Minnesota's hatchery program has proven much too costly as well as ineffective, current policy has focused on wild fish management. The good folks at the Natural Resource office encouraged me to give their waters a try despite the dismal conditions. It was obvious that they still believed the remnant populations of wild steelhead that inhabit Minnesota's tributaries were well worth an angler's effort.

Armed with fresh insight and renewed enthusiasm, the search for fishable water along Minnesota's north shore began; but reality set back in soon enough with one glance of the muddy Knife River. Although several other tributaries were not off-color, the raging aspect of most certainly kept me on the road without even stringing up the eight weight. It was the Baptism River, though, that lived up to its name, giving my beleaguered spirit a rebirth. Despite copious amounts of rich, reddish-tea-colored but clear water, there were actually some good pockets and bends that could be effectively fished. In addition, the first natural barrier occurred a good distance upstream, allowing for the possibility to explore this uncommonly beautiful piece of water. Nightfall on a particularly cold May evening postponed my efforts until the following morning. With a lake full of thirty-five degree water influencing local temperatures, it seemed obvious why most folks in Duluth sported permanent scowls.

I don't normally mind breaking ice out of guides; sometimes that is part of the Great Lakes steelhead experience. But it was almost June, and waiting until the morning temperature was at least above freezing before heading down to the river seemed the appropriate tactic. By nine o'clock, the sun had cast some relatively warm streaks of light through the shadows of the shallow canyon, just perfect for steelheading. And finding a deep shelf with a flat tailout provided a rare opportunity to fish for awhile. Within the next few hours, I hooked and lost my first—and only—Minnesota steelhead. It was a spunky but characteristically small fish. Even though it threw the hook on the third jump, my excitement far outweighed the disappointing loss.

The realization, however, that fishable water on the Baptism was also extremely limited hit home an hour later when I was dangerously standing in a chest-deep flow trying to work an unreachable pocket with absolutely no success. Futility is sometimes an overwhelming form of truth. After a near spill, getting out of the water and walking back to my vehicle seemed to be the only judicious thing to do. It was then I met a senior Minnesotan who was eating lunch in his truck after a morning of fishing. Unbelievably, the elderly gentleman even cracked a smile when I approached. His name was Merlin.

"You must have caught a fish?" I asked somewhat whimsically.

"No," he laughed, "I haven't caught a fish here in years. I should amend that statement though. I haven't really had too many opportunities to get out fishing over the past fifteen years. But now that I'm retired, I intend to make up for far too much time of too little fly fishing."

After exchanging details of our morning adventures, I asked, "To your knowledge, how has the steelhead fishing been the past decade?"

"You just don't hear much about it anymore," Merlin replied. "When I moved here in 1957, the locals used to brag about keeping as many as fifty rainbows in a day for the smokehouse. Even back then, I could not figure the wisdom behind that kind of fishery abuse. But it didn't seem to faze them; it never does. Over the years, rainbow numbers declined and people started to clamor for more fish. They never did seem to make the connection. All they do is complain about the fishing that they had a hand in destroying!"

It was difficult not to appreciate Merlin's candor and astute assessment of the present-day status of Minnesota's steelhead. There was no question he had identified one factor that seems to be a common problem throughout the entire Great Lakes. This is a special resource with limited capabilities, but try explaining that to those whose primary source of enlightenment comes from a can of Bud.

"I really like fishing the small streams around here for brookies," Merlin continued. "Years ago, my son and I would often hike the Manitou River from sun up to dark, catching and releasing many fish up to fourteen inches. Those were the days! Nowadays, well, there's too darn many people on the rivers who don't seem to care about much."

I was really enjoying the conversation, especially since I had not casually talked to a soul other than a brief encounter with the fish and game folks (my dog doesn't count) in the four-and-a-half days that it took to get to this place from Montana. "How long have you been fly fishing?" I quizzed him further.

"A long time, but I really put away my spinning rods forever when I read *Trout Fishing* by Joe Brooks in 1973."

I looked at him in amazement. Excusing myself for a minute, I walked over to my rig and dug through a pile of notes to find the story I had just completed about my grandfather which I called "Gramps." I then cited the references to Joe Brooks's *Trout Fishing* in that piece.

Although Merlin didn't seem too moved by the apparent coincidence, he remarked, "Yup. Joe Brooks was my hero." Again I showed him another sentence where I referred to both Gramps and Joe Brooks as my heroes also. With that, Merlin chuckled a bit. You never know when you are going to bump into another soul spirit, but at that moment I felt I had known this fellow for a lifetime. Upon going our separate ways, I asked Merlin where his next venture would lead.

"An old friend wants to walk the Manitou in a few weeks, you know, for old times sake. But I don't know if I have the endurance to pull that one off anymore."

"Do it over a few days," I said. "You could camp along the way. That really sounds like something you need to do."

"I'd really like to do it again with my son, but he's down south now raising a family. You know how that is. But you are right; I do need to make that hike again. Thank you for the encouragement and the fine discussion." Merlin then bid me good-bye. I wished him many happy fishing days throughout his retirement. He nodded, and then smiled, as he drove back toward Duluth.

Up the road, I reflected over lunch at Sven and Olie's Pizza Parlor. I could hardly pass up the opportunity to eat at Sven and Olie's, given the urgings plastered on successive billboards along the way. "It's goot fer yew" was the caption uttered by a robust appearing nordic woman wearing one of those Norsemen hats with the protruding horns. Considering the winter-like May conditions, I figured the only thing "goot fer me, ya" was to get the hell out of Minnesota. So while wondering if the origins of pizza could possibly be traced back to Viking explorers, I made the decision to continue on toward the border. I'd be there in an hour.

Back to reality. The customs agent proceeded to examine my rods, my reels, my vest, my clothes, my fishing notes and books. Although it should have been clearly evident that my angling intentions were firmly corroborated by a truckload of well-used fishing paraphernalia, I then took a calculated risk and made a bold suggestion that could possibly speed the process along—or land me on a chain gang.

"Check out chapter nineteen in that book, *Great Lakes Steelhead*, by Bob Linsenman and Steve Nevala. Although the entire chapter is about my brother, Rick, my name is mentioned right there,"— I pointed—"on page two fourty-four."

"Oh, so you *are* here to fish for steelhead," he stated in a half-interested sort of way. "Have anything else to declare?"

I bit my lip real hard. At that point, Canada didn't look so beautiful anyway.

A minute later, I was on my way while evaluating the significance of the journey to this point. I'd like to say fishing improved over the next few days, but for all the effort, every river in Ontario was at extreme flood stage as well. Steelheading is like that; therein lies its beauty and its curse. Anywhere they swim, so many factors have to come together at the exact right moment to encounter one of these magnificent creatures. When it happens, there is nothing more thrilling! And when it doesn't... Well, that's the life of the steelheader.

Then again, I *do declare* there is more to a fishing trip than catching fish. But don't tell that to the folks at the border.

And another thing. Make damn sure you take some beer.

The River

Those summer days of youth—how they seemed so perfect! Baseball, swimming and fishing.... What more could a kid want! They were lemonade kind of days. You know, the kind that blend reality and fantasy, hopes and dreams, into a collage of memories—bits and pieces collected from a past when times seemed better than they actually were. The cotton candy clouds gliding through a sky of blue, a tepid breeze whisking comforting solace in the shade of an old oak, and not a care in the world. Ah, life was good!

"Mantle swings—" Mel Allen's magic drew my undivided attention to the radio that delivered every Yankee game to the inner sanctum of my bedroom. "—and there it goes. Going, going, gone. How about that!" I was enthralled. And I so much wanted to be like "the Mick." To demonstrate that commitment, I even learned to switch-hit by the time I was ten. I so much wanted to play in the major leagues, too. That's all I really dreamed about, and that's all I thought about when I frequently spent endless non-baseball hours fishing the Niagara River—gazing upon the surface of glass, sniffing the oddest of odors. The mighty Niagara carried the contents of Lake Erie around Grand Island, where I lived, over Niagara Falls and finally into Lake Ontario. The River, as the locals called it, was my friend; a sort of mantra where the fine line between imagination and real life seemed to blur the looking glass of time and space. It was there the secrets of meaningful expression flowed by, concealed in the passing waters, waiting, perhaps, to be hooked on my garden worm offering.

Pick-up ball games in the countryside where I grew up usually consisted of three or four kids per side. We played on a makeshift diamond constructed by several parents in the grown-over fields behind our homes. A pride permeated the houses that were built shortly after WWII. Neighbors got along, and parents nurtured their children in a fantasyland of family involvement. So what if ground balls would careen erratically from one clump of uneven earth to another, and sometimes off a nose. We were playing on a labor of love. In the outfield patches of wild strawberries, every bouncer created sweet fragrances that added pink tones to the multistained cowhide wrapping something resembling a hardball. Those days, all things were rosy!

Pity the poor soul, however, who "yanked" a fly to deep left or short right. With a muted thud, or sometimes a sucking squish, the ill-fated ball would plop into a cattail marsh—the wet, soggy ooze that would devour baseballs like a giant vacuum. We all feared the swamp as if peril awaited any unsuspecting intruder who dared venture into that black hole. And to be so unfortunate as to do the yanking! We played by the "you lose it, you find it" rules governing sandlot ball games, probably written in the early days of the sport by Doubleday himself. But sometimes the yanker would get lucky and emerge from the quagmire with water-soaked ball in hand, looking as if he just had cheated death in sneakers caked with mud and angry red-winged blackbirds buzz bombing the top of his head. Since we had only one extra ball, and the cover was usually ripped off that one—or just hanging by a few threads—options were few. Over the years we all learned the prudence of hitting to straight away center field.

"Going, going," I would say under my breath as another of my firmly stroked fly balls would set sail well into the oblivion of the center field bushes. "Gone!" Yes! A country mile! The Big Kahuna, the Mick, the Say-Hey Kid all rolled into one! My cronies would marvel, all seven of them—okay, so two of them were girls—but in my mind, I was the best. Trotting around the bases, the crowds cheered (actually it was just Snoozy, the cantankerous mutt that belonged to the first baseman). But I had visions. There weren't the lucrative contracts back then, just baseball cards, and a chance at bubblegum immortality. Who would trade any amount of money for an opportunity like that!

I guess I should have suspected there was something wrong with the River all along. In the spring when the alewives piled into two-foot-high windrows along the River's shoreline, the maggot-retching stench of rotting fish would waft the quarter of a mile through the slightly opened window of my bedroom. I had no way of knowing that nothing about this was natural—not the alewives, not the death. I was just a kid, what could I know? I did know one thing: it wasn't any more pleasant along the River in the summertime either. But the endless procession of dead, discolored, fungused fish was intriguing. For if nothing else, the floaters always provided a continuous supply of specimens to test one's skill of identification.

Once, while walking along a sandy shoreline and poking at the carcasses of countless fish that would regularly wash up with the algae and driftwood, one barefooted step revealed a sickening soft spot on the beach followed by a welling up of stinking puslike goo that squished over my foot. It was the putrid remains of a ten pound carp buried about two inches below the surface of the sand. In one movement I was in the water! Washing and scrubbing the oily mush that slithered through my toes gagged me with disgust. I'm not sure, but I think it was then a light went on and, most probably, a cynic was born.

Despite it all, I loved the River. I heard rumors that Lake Erie was dying, but I really didn't know what that meant. I saw the dead fish and, sometimes, when there were health alerts, we couldn't swim in the waters of the Niagara either. Unbelievably, there were still some fish alive in the River at that time, and I loved to fish for them. First with my grandfather, then with my cousin Paul, but after a few years, primarily by myself. Fishing became a solitary pursuit, a refuge from the common pains of growing up. The River came to be my mentor and my guide. It spirited a lifelong quest to understand completely the forces of fishing and, ultimately, the mysterious joys of mastering the sport on a fly rod. And in many waiting rooms both *Outdoor Life* and *Sports Afield* fed my dreams, especially when I made those regular visits to the orthodontist to get the hardware in my mouth adjusted.

The morning ball game had just ended when Paul asked if there were any takers for a refreshing dip in the River. The Lake Erie region always provided moderate weather in the summer, but sometimes the humidity was overbearing. Not that kids notice things like sticky and sultry; we just knew it was a great day for swimming. But I had a problem—it came in the form of my mother. Ever since I needed five stitches to close a wound on my heel from a piece of strewn glass concealed in the sand during the previous year, I hadn't been allowed to enter the River again. Even then, she warned me beforehand that I would hurt myself swimming in the River. In her mind, it was dangerous. The image of the raging Falls a few miles downriver didn't help my case either. I hated that, for every time she predicted something would happen—it would! "Don't go outside without your hat, or else!" or "Don't pick on your sister, or else!" The "or else" would usually result in a cold or a bloody nose. This time I did ask, beg, and plead. And, this time, good old Mom gave in. I was fortunate as well; the permission came with no prophetic "or else." I felt blessed.

Johnny Joe, the owner of Snoozy, was the only other kid interested in taking up cousin Paul on his proposal, so off the three of us went on our rusty old bicycles to the corner where our road met the River. The water looked so inviting, but there was always a creepy feeling whenever any part of my body touched the River's water. The slimy algae, the floating fish, and a pervasive smell were discomforting, but these distractions did not deter us from our mission. Into the River we jumped. All was good!

Imagination can be a potent force. Whenever my legs bumped into something below the water's surface, goosebumps ran up the back of my neck. In fact, my hair would have stood up for sure if it had been any longer than brush bristle. I conjured up dead bodies or the last of the four-foot toothy muskellunge, but the slime growth and bloated fish with gray fuzz were bad enough. And some of these fish even exhibited this hideous condition while still swimming slowly in circles before dying. When my cousin found a near dead, twelve-inch bullhead floating by, he seemed compelled by an unexplainable urge to do something unthinkable.

A bullhead isn't the prettiest of creatures. Being among the most resilient, though, certainly its river-wide demise should have symbolized something. It has smooth skin like a shark, with a horizontal but toothless mouth that predominates a big, flat head accented by sensory whiskers symmetrically hanging from each corner of its bullhead lips. The tip of the dorsal and pectoral fins are well-armed with a projectile, which, if the fish is mishandled, can leave the handler with a very painful puncture.

As a playful prank, Paul hoisted this grotesque creature out of the water, thumb and forefinger barely grasping its tail. Then, in the same motion, he innocently lobbed it in Johnny Joe's direction. He wasn't thinking in terms of mini harpoons. So when that fuzzy, mostly dead, but still wiggling bullhead struck Johnnie Joe in the arm, we were aghast! Coming to rest about the vicinity of the smallpox scar, it hung there by the dorsal fin like a dart sticking smack dab in the middle of a bulls-eye. Frozen in the moment, there stood a terrified Johnny Joe in knee-deep goop with a writhing bullhead attached to his appendage. Paul and I laughed, but Johnny Joe's look of shock turned to fear, and then to panic. Extracting the fish, he frantically charged out of the water. We could hear his cries fade off into the distance as he ran the entire distance home.

Johnny Joe was okay, but I couldn't sleep that night—Catholic guilt, I suppose—for laughing. Something wasn't right, but I just didn't know what. The natural process was disintegrating before my youthful eyes. But to me, this was nature. I wasn't thinking at the time about the truth. Although the Great Lakes have been in existence for only 12,000 years, about the same period attributed to the evolution of modern-thinking man, the best our forefathers had to offer the youth of my day was a river full of dead bullheads. What gives? The human influence in the Great Lakes basin dated back only a few hundred years. So much for good stewardship! All I could think of when I closed my eyes was that bullhead clinging to my friend's arm like a crucifix.

Growing up includes many realizations. The saddest for me occurred when my major league baseball career couldn't get past high school. It was a simple case of a big fish from a small pond getting devoured by bigger fish from the ocean. Those strawberry fields of my younger years weren't forever, as I hoped they would be. And when Lake Erie's death was confirmed while I was still in high school, as well, it wasn't sadness, but anger that overwhelmed my senses. After that proclamation, I rarely visited the River for many years afterward. A few years later, when the Viet Nam fiasco spread the tentacles that sucked all good sense out of a nation, and well aware that I could die without ever becoming an adult, I realized that, yes, childhood was most definitely over.

Since those days, the Clean Water Act has inspired a massive revitalization effort that has resulted in the restoration of Lake Erie and the Niagara River to a healthy, but impaired, water system. When it comes to nature, I suppose half a loaf is better than nothing. Since those days I have become a staunch environmentalist, as well, and I make no excuses or apologies. And since those days, I have also become a fly fisherman in pursuit of the earth's purest reaches—partly to escape, and partly to recapture, the past. I think constantly of the meaning of nature and man's role in reshaping it, and while I'd like to catch trout as a mindless process of avoiding life's encumbrances, I am plagued by visions of bullheads.

What is nature anyway? Sure, wilderness, the earthly paradigm of Godlike perfection, comes to mind as the quintessential untainted expression of the notion, but nature must also be expressed reflecting man's existence. Equilibrium and balance, as well as biodiversity, are key ingredients defining the concept. Beauty, unspoiled, unfragmented, unfenced, undeveloped, etc. are also characteristics applied to the term "nature." It is wind, it is rain, it is birds, it is animals, it is man. Ultimately, it is all life and all things living in harmony; a give and take, a compromise of sorts, to ensure that, indeed, the sum of the parts adds up to some greater all-encompassing spirit. Conversely, if any one element gets out of balance in this complexity of forces, there are universal laws of "reckoning" wreaked upon the offender. That's what nature does because that's what nature is.

We all seem to long for the same things—a quiet river, a peaceful mountain, a soothing beach, and solitude. Yet when it comes to the natural elements that fuel these dreams, the facts just don't add up. In a society that is pro-growth and pro-development, we all seem to be too willing to sell out nature a little here and a little there, from every side and every angle, to further promote everything we escape into natural settings to avoid. One step forward, two steps back, nature as we know it is being squeezed out of existence. Never mind the lessons learned from the Great Lakes, or a thousand times over elsewhere. The truth is harsh, and the human being finds plenty of excuses not to face it. These days, the truth amounts to conveniently manipulated facts that fit any situation to justify any profitable cause. Gone is the soul-searching, gut-wrenching introspection responsible for revelations leading to philosophical wisdom that is the real truth. It is instant gratification—do now, think later—that drives the engine forward.

I hate to be sanctimonious, but one tends to see things while standing in a river. One gets a sense of where things are going as the all-encompassing water moves on by. A recent article in the *New York Times* indicates by its title that "The Population Explosion is Over" and, while we should all be jumping for joy with that announcement, don't let complacency take over just yet. In 1968, Paul Ehrlich predicted that earth's human population would exceed sustainability topping eleven billion by 2050. The author of the article, Ben J. Wattenburg, recently refigured the statistic using updated data. He calculated that the population should stabilize at only eight billion or so by 2050, and then drop. That's still up another few billion in the next fifty years. Good news? It's like learning you've got cancer in just one lung instead of two. Consider also that since 1981, in the United States alone, we have lost over one half of our agricultural land to development. The same sprawl is fragmenting our deserts, wetlands, foothills, forests, and mountains, not to mention the residual waste it takes to fuel such "progress." Additionally, the atmosphere continues to lose ozone, and there is only so much usable, fresh water to go around. Just do the math! I can't ignore these facts when I go fishing. When I close my eyes, I can't help seeing fuzzy bullheads. And I have to wonder if that's what *we'll* be passing on to future generations.

The way I see it, there are two courses of action. One is to do nothing. The other is to make the effort to learn what can be done, and then live a life reflecting those concerns. I'm selfish; I'll admit it. I long to see wild salmonids swimming forever in the most natural of settings, and I promise to challenge any effort that threatens this desire. There is an undeniable force that draws many of us to nature, yet nothing rankles more than the environmentalist who dares make the general public aware of these glaring trends. And while we all long for secluded places and quiet retreats, we readily acquiesce to the movements that aim to transform the entire planet into a theme park—a push-button convenience requiring no participation and no effort—while systematically eliminating all ability to connect with the inner, vibrant, meaningful soul of the earth in the process.

The house still stands where I grew up. The neighborhood hasn't changed much either. The old baseball diamond is now wooded over. And the River doesn't stink anymore. Although baseball cards mean nothing to me these days, I still allow myself to dream now and then, "Going, going..."

When it comes to nature, I'll admit the lines are blurred. While Lake Erie's water is crystal-clear these days, non-native species of Pacific salmonids thrive alongside some of the re-established indigenous fish populations. Bird life abounds, as well. The entire Great Lakes basin is a system of compromise, perhaps seeking balance with the influences of mankind factored into the complex equation of environmental soundness.

A few years ago, I was fishing the lower Niagara in a section of turbulent water well below the Falls when a fish viciously grabbed my fly. As it flew wildly through the air, I could see it was big, it was silver, and it was hot. Running to keep up with it, my line was leaving the reel faster than I thought. Through the fly line and into the backing, the big steelhead kept jumping its way back toward Lake Ontario until I heard the pop signaling, I am embarrassed to say, the loss of the entire spool of line. "...gone. How about that!" The weight forward floater plus one hundred fifty yards of backing showed up the next day stretched along the shore—minus the steelhead, of course, which obviously got its wish.

I thought for a moment as I stared at my empty reel. Hmmm... Sure beats dead bullheads.

McDuff's Knutt

Twin Bridges of Madison County—sounds like a darn good title for a book! It was only back in the eighties, but already the recollections from that time radiate all the phantasmagorical charm of Garrison Keillor's Lake Wobegon days. The ageless dimension of yesteryear projects an eternal presence of days gone by; fantasy becomes the reality, and the spiritual breeze that connects us to the past whispers eternal bits of truth hidden within the fabled stories. There was Mac's Grocery Store and the Ruby Valley Hardware; Marge officiously ran the post office, and Berta, the town's perfect grandma, always shared a smile and some pertinent pearl of wisdom reflecting the years of calling this small Montana town her home. Of course, the escapades of the few town drunks spiced the stories of the local wags, as well.

In the almanac of towns, Twin Bridges has always been a one blinker; that is, one timely blink of the eye on Montana's Highway 41 and you've missed it. While *two bridges* of Madison County, Montana, do define this mini-ranching community—one over the Beaverhead River "that runs through it" and the other that crosses the Big Hole on its outskirts—the business center of three bars and assorted empty buildings usually urges most visitors to just keep moving on. For years, the area's fishing was a best-kept secret and, in those days, only the serious angler pursuing a day on the fickle Big Hole River would occasionally stop into "Twin," as the townsfolk call it. Some sought repast, possibly a Hawaiian burger at the Blue Anchor Bar and Grill. Most could not pass up a visit to Scott Waldie's Four Rivers Fishing Company. For decades, this revered shop catered to the needs of the passing fly fisher during southwestern Montana's ephemeral fishing season, which usually sandwiches itself between high water on one end and a blizzard on the other. After selling a fly or two and giving out some sage fishing info, Scott, a reputable outdoor writer, would return to his typewriter (turned word processor in the late eighties) to continue writing about the colorful characters he regularly encountered living in Twin Bridges. We all graced the pages of his stories at one time or another.

On a side street across the way, the R. L. Winston Rod Company obscurely blended into its colorful, but tired-looking surroundings in a modest sort of way. The townsfolk and surrounding grizzled ranchers could never quite figure out the allure of this manufacturing shop. The concept of paying hundreds of dollars for a "fishing pole" was puzzling to the hard-working native Montanan who was proud of the bailing wire and duct tape approach to keeping the world, as he knew it, intact. But from near and far, the cultists would come to pay homage to the business that made the green rod so important to their existence. In their minds, this rod was the magic wand responsible for raising a mere fishing experience to another meaningful level along with their transcended beings. Whether it was the passion for perfection, the commitment to the dry fly, or the friendly responsiveness to all believers of the product, the devoted Winston following rivaled, in a small way, that of the Grateful Dead. Though this business's market share was small potatoes compared to the rest of the fishing industry, its loyal band of disciples set the company apart from all its competition. The locals could hardly understand it, but somehow they realized that the life Winston breathed into the community most certainly kept cobwebs from choking the town council.

The employees at the rod shop were a talented group of creative individuals and misfits. Many had gathered in the area while shunning the social norms of the era to carve out a meager existence in the quest of living life in harmony with Montana's splendor. Unlike the many migrants of this past decade who cannot derive satisfaction out of life in the Big Sky State unless it is controlled, fenced, locked up, and then posted, these remnant renegades of the late sixties believed in honesty, integrity and the freedom of wide open spaces. The virtues of this eccentric gathering became the foundation as the company expanded upon its reputation of excellence that had been nurtured for many decades. Among the rules of employment were two of notable significance: only build rods on days you felt like building them; and, if the bugs were hatching and the fish rising, go fishing! There was intensity in those days tempered with congeniality and a firm commitment to quality, but when the Mother's Day caddis began slapping the windows on the warm, sunny days of late April, there was the flexibility to bolt down to the river. After all, wasn't that what a company that built rods was all about?

Life in a small town is defined by its simple folks and simple pleasures, and there's not much that goes on without everybody knowing about it. These parameters suit most folks just fine, and because everything, good and bad, is shared to a certain degree by all, the social operative is more akin to the workings of an extended family unit. Part of this shared experience was the character known to us all as McDuff.

Unlike most townies, McDuff was of the four-legged persuasion, a Scottish terrior by birth, but it would have been difficult to convince McDuff of that. In fact, this "dog" could have run for mayor and most probably would have won. With the swagger and confidence of Newt Gingrich, McDuff patrolled the streets, entering any establishment that suited his fancy. McDuff had a daily routine that made sense only to him, but as he made his rounds, the Winston shop was a regular stop on his route. Twice a week, doughnuts and their accompanying doughnut holes were imported from the bakery located in the neighboring town of Sheridan. Without fail, McDuff would be positioned at the exact place and time every Tuesday and Thursday to collect his share of the booty as the goodies made their way into the building. This, he must have figured, was worthy enough compensation for services rendered as self-proclaimed neighborhood enforcer. After collecting, McDuff would wait at the door, and then, upon its opening, depart with a cocky strut to continue his dutiful chores.

McDuff became as much an ingredient of the green rod's complex essence as did the conversations around the shop about water conditions, fish populations, and the effects of the drought on our blue ribbon fisheries. Whether it was on the phone, dealing with walk-in clients, or just amongst ourselves, the talk always seemed to get around to fishing—as well it should. Glenn Brackett and Tom Morgan were hands-on owners, and they were always available—unless they were on a river somewhere. As an astute itinerant fly fisherman with an extensive background in fishery biology, Glenn's views were always illuminating. Tom Morgan's lifetime involvement with the Madison River and his visionary elevation of a fly fishing product to the level of usable art is now legendary. Add this wisdom to the insightful expertise of production manager Jerry Siem on any topic from his world-class casting experiences to catching bluegills in the backbays of the Mississippi River, and a person could have earned a master's degree in fly fishology. More advanced degrees were available, as well, if one paid attention to the wealth of knowledge that regularly passed through the hallowed halls of the humble rod shop each season.

Though Jerry was known more for his ability to cast a full fly line (without a rod!), he was less recognized as an innovator and creator of new fly patterns—a talent in which he quietly took great pride. Often scoffing the "off the rack" variety fly, he believed that most flies displayed commercially were dressed to catch the attention of a fisherman, not a fish. "When was the last time you saw a good-looking bug?" he would ask, adding, "If you look closely, most bugs are pretty ugly, and that's what most fish see."

It was quite obvious that Jerry had spent much time along some of the world's finest rivers formulating this philosophy. And when you saw some of his flies, it was also quite obvious that he practiced what he preached. By design, he intentionally put together some of the world's ugliest flies. In fact, if he would have thrown a handful of them on a countertop somewhere, the first impulse would have been to immediately reach for a can of Raid—and to Jerry, that would have been a great compliment.

To some, the art of tying flies is a craft, and to others, the craft of tying flies is an art. Such subjectivity is the magical thread that *ties* many of the intangible digressions of fly fishing together. Everyone I know approaches fly tying from different angles. For instance, to address the persnickety risers in many streams east of the Mississippi, my brother, Rick, has learned to tie imitations with meticulous exactitude to appease the most snobby residents of the eminent eastern trouteries. The wisdom of this approach became perplexingly clear during an emergence of *emphemerella dorothea* one evening years ago on the Delaware's West Branch. Preciseness was what the fish wanted, but they didn't get it from me!

When it comes to Glenn Brackett, his approach to fly tying is an allegorical statement of life as he sees it. Glenn spent many of his earlier years as a professional fly tyer, and much of his "spare" time was devoted to developing *the* definitive dry fly. Striving for simplicity, he studied colors, materials and profiles for years; finally, all of his efforts culminated in the one-fly-fits-all design. The

Oneness Fly, as I call it, works remarkably well in a myriad of situations, and it is the only fly he has used for years. He officially ties this same fly in several different sizes—that is its only variation. Glenn believes the art of tying flies, like everything we do right down to drinking a glass of water, can be a Zen experience. Though this approach to the tying bench may not be the key to eternal happiness, it may lead down the path of contented peacefulness to a life of peaceful contentment, or so I'm inspired to believe.

Another innovator I've long admired is Butte's master tier and the Big Hole River's treasured friend, George Grant. In the Pott's tradition, George has woven his masterpieces for decades, one strand at a time, in what can only be termed a true labor of love. Paul Redfern of Butte learned many of George's secrets and passed them on to Todd Collins, also of Butte. Todd has taken it upon himself to keep this tradition alive in his beautiful replications of George's creations, and Tom Harman of Sheridan has spent hours learning the craft locally. Just observing the painstaking devotion to produce one of these beauties adds yet another dimension to the many expressive levels this avocation can take. Considering that each fly takes at least a few hours to create, fishing with one of them would take a lot of nerve. But if you dared to reduce this creation to such a mundane level of pragmatic use, stripping naked to retrieve it would be a consideration once the fly hung up on the inevitable overhanging willow or submerged hidden log.

My approach to this important phase of the sport is purely utilitarian. Along with my box of standard flies, accumulated as a part of the obligatory winter tying ritual, are the flies *de jour* pertinently tied precisely minutes before my regular visits to the plethora of local fishing venues. That way, I could be armed with exactly what is needed to match hatching events occurring on our rivers each day. However, no matter how many flies I've tied immediately before heading out the door, I usually end up with exactly two of them remaining by the end of the day—this apparently dictated by Murphy's Law of Fly Tying. Whether it be in a willow, tall grass, fish's mouth, or just plain falling off the patch on my vest seemingly designed for that purpose, count them by day's end: two left. These are then placed into the aforementioned utility box for future use as backups, and thus my collection grows.

Deciding to put the two fly theory to the test, I once whipped out a dozen elk hairs, serendipities, and LaFontaine emergers in combination before the drive to the Madison River's Westfork area for a July day of caddis fun. Of course, I lost the first fly immediately on a nice fish attached to 6x tippet, but I had eleven more laying loosely in one of those courtesy plastic boxes from the Four River's shop stashed safely in a special vest pocket, so I wasn't concerned. Under the dark scowl of an approaching thunderstorm and determined to beat this dreaded curse, I cut back the leader and, to be safe, added 3x tippet just as the rain began to thrash the river's surface. The fish started to rise feverishly, and since I couldn't contain myself, I reached for the guarded box neatly tucked into a secure pocket. Once out, I carefully opened it at the exact moment a dynamic gust of wind belched from the north, blowing the contents somewhere within a mile radius of the river. I did manage to find two flies, and they lasted the rest of the day.

One day in early May, Jerry called me over to his area of the shop and confided that he had probably just engineered his finest fly ever, and "it works great!" Jerry could hardly contain his enthusiasm as he searched his shirt pocket for the prototype while, at the same time, relating the great successes of the prior evening floating the Jefferson River. Jerry's home was on the Jefferson, and he had tremendous faith in its ability to produce fish. There was one thing for sure: on sunny days in May, it did produce prolific hatches of early golden stoneflies and even larger numbers of a smaller *isoperla* stonefly that we lumped into the "yellow sally" category. When he finally placed The Fly into the palm of my hand, I gawked at an unusually sleek but bushy creation. It sported a yellow body, a sweep of lemon wood duck flank feathers combined with another ingredient of unknown origins, neatly packaged and framed by just the right amount of grizzly hackle. Jerry was right. It was a swell looking fly! He was also quick to add that the fly was virtually indestructible; he used Super Glue during every phase of its construction.

"Do you want to try a few?" He asked. Since it has never been my practice to turn down an opportunity for a free fly or two, I gladly accepted the offer. It would probably be a few days, though, until he tied up a batch. When he asked how many, I told him that four would be a good number since I would probably lose two the first evening out. "By the way," I inquired, "what do you call it?" Jerry smiled. "McDuff's Nut!"

Why "McDuff's Nut?" I wondered. Certainly this was a fine tribute to the shop's loyal mascot/security guard and the likely semantic segue to this canine's passion for doughnuts. Or, I surmised, it could be an anatomical reference to those parts responsible for this dog's brash machismo. When I asked Jerry, he remarked mysteriously, "You know that unknown ingredient I mentioned?" Though I could never figure the real connection, from that day on I checked McDuff for little snips of missing hair. Officially, the fly became known as McDuff's Knutt, to further confuse the etymology of its title.

When Jerry delivered the four flies a few days later, the early May conditions on the Jefferson remained ideal. Cool nights, warm days, and no rain kept the river clear and the fish looking up. The daily smattering of stoneflies stimulated the interest of every fish within eyesight of any natural bug floating the river's surface—*whoof*, it was gone! Within the first hour, several fish rose to McDuff's Knutt with authority. After landing a few rainbows and a fair-sized brown, I got to thinking that maybe Jerry had created a monster.

Do you remember in math or science class there was always this nebulous term called a constant? This was the value in a formula that always remained the same, but not even the teacher could explain why. For example, pi (π) always equalled 3.14285...etc. and this term would end up in everything you ever needed to know about a circle. A constant always seemed to me like a cosmic fudge factor, but I guess that's just the way the universe works. Without describing any of the details, by the end of that first evening on "the Jeff," I had only two McDuff's Knutts remaining. Need I say more?

I got down to the Jeff several times during the next few weeks, and nursing those last two flies was a chore. Jerry would have freely supplied more for the cause, but it was a matter of pride not to appear the desperate mooch. My feeble attempts to duplicate his creation at my own vise were often judged inadequate by the fish, but they did fool the Laws of Murphy. After using and losing a few of my inferior imitations each afternoon, at the appropriate time I shrewdly pulled out a genuine McDuff's and casually exchanged it for my version. Tying it, just to be safe, to a 2x tippet, my intentions were to trick the goblins responsible for gobbling my flies. The tactic routinely worked, and the fly caught fish after fish. Jerry was right about another thing; McDuff's Knutt was indestructible. It continued to float like a cork daily, and there was never a hackle or hair out of place, even after hooking many fish in two weeks.

Then one day the unthinkable occurred. It was just a lapse of judgment, but instead of carefully placing McDuff's into a safe box at the end of the previous outing, I attached it to the patch on my vest. What was I thinking!? Upon pulling the garment stuffed to the gills with everything imaginable out of my rig the next time out, the fly was no longer there. It may seem silly, but guarding those last two Knutts became an obsession, and now one of them was gone.

A thorough check of the truck's cab revealed no fly, but by then the day's calm was disrupted by a spring thunderstorm complete with winds, hail, and a significant temperature drop. One hour and a long nap later, the weather barely settled enough to salvage a few hours of very late afternoon activity; that is, if the cold rain didn't scare the river's inhabitants. Carefully I tied the last McDuff's Knutt onto my tippet and headed for the water. Clearing the leader and fly line from the guides of my Winston five-weight with a few false casts, I was about to release the line toward the water. Just then this overwhelmingly sinking sensation produced a hollow feeling in the pit of my stomach. At that exact moment I simultaneously realized that my last McDuff's was no longer tied to the end of the leader. Montana's long, coarse grasses from the previous year can cut leaders like a razor blade; and I spent a substantial amount of dwindling daylight crawling through it looking for that fly. But it was a futile effort. The goblins had spoken. I gathered my rod and reeled in the empty line. Defeated, I headed back home wondering what rerun was on TV that night.

I didn't fish the Jefferson again for several days. The stoneflies continued to progressively unfold up into the Big Hole along with the typical early season caddis activity. When the water warms enough to trigger the Mother's Day grannoms, however, murky snowmelt isn't usually too far behind. Since springtime conditions in the northern Rockies are not able to be relied upon from one day to the next, taking advantage of this phenomenon normally translates into "just doing it" when the opportunity presents itself. In other words, since it was happening on the Big Hole, that's where I was. My choice of flies turned to the standard caddis fare appropriate for the conditions, although there was still some interest in the odd stonefly. Jerry even volunteered to replenish my supply of McDuff's Knutts with the original recipe, but by the time he got around to tying a few, and then forgetting them at home, the spring runoff had begun within those few days. The day before the conditions changed drastically, I headed back to the Jefferson.

The late afternoon sun was just beginning to cast May shadows upon the river in the warmth of a day that had approached the sixty degree range, but hadn't quite made it. Stepping into the Jefferson, the apparent lack of bug life revealed a feeling that this section of river had most likely passed its prime hatch time for this particular part of the season. And because of the impending runoff, the next significant period for dry flies would not be until late June. After spending a few hours not even moving a fish with a variety of non-McDuff's, I got to thinking that it was about time to work down to where I had parked my vehicle along the river, and head for home. In the slow progression of step, cast and wait, step, cast, and wait, my eye caught a glimpse of an angler who had just played and landed a fish a few hundred yards below at the head of the next run. It was tough to make out, but it appeared that he had tossed the fish into the bushes. A few minutes later, he repeated the process. And then a few minutes later, it all happened again.

I am not much of a busybody, but I will lay claim to being a self-appointed guardian of our rivers, especially when a certain activity looks suspicious. There is a catch-and-release only regulation for all rainbow trout on the Jefferson, and as I casually made my way to the active fisherman, he was playing and landing a rather chunky rainbow. Without even seeing me, the young man, decked out in patched rubber hip boots and a crumpled, disintegrating vest, released the bow back into the river. Getting up to him, I peaked casually into the bushes and found a pile of whitefish, shaded and lying on some wet grass. When he saw me, he volunteered, "A good mess for smoking, don't you think?" My faith in humanity was restored.

Just as we began to politely chat—*whop!*—another nice rainbow grabbed his fly and took off straight toward the middle of the slow-moving pool. In the ensuing battle, he expressed a deep-seated disappointment that he wasn't able to keep rainbows anymore. We discussed the reasons why, and he understood that he would rather be catching and releasing than not catching at all. Fishing pressure and the intermittent lack of water in the summer had taken a toll on the historic populations of rainbow in the Jeff, and these new regulations were designed to benefit fish populations. As he gratefully released that next fish, he admitted to no complaints. I wish I could say the same, since I had yet to stir even the smallest of fish.

Not that I thought it particularly mattered, but I asked him out of curiosity to what fly he attributed his remarkable success. He responded by saying it was the oddest thing he had ever seen, and then he pulled it out of the water and held it up for my perusal. It couldn't be! "Holy Rod Serling," I gasped! This had to be a joke, or maybe a ghost, but at that moment there was no question in my mind that I had just stepped into the Twilight Zone. There, tied to approximately a two-foot tippet of twenty pound monofilament was an original McDuff's Knutt. "I don't know what there is about this fly," the angler confided, "but I have been using it for the last several evenings and, man, have I caught fish! I finally put it on a heavy leader so as not to lose it."

It took a few minutes for me to come back to reality, and at that moment logic kicked into gear. I could only assume that he had found *the* very McDuff lost from my botched escapade of over a week ago. When words finally returned to my lips, I regaled the gentleman with my sad story. Pointing to the area on which his four-wheel drive sat, I told him it was about there that I had lost it. My words must have been convincing, for he actually offered to give the fly back. I laughingly suggested that for some reason it appeared he was meant to have it by Powers much greater than I; far be it from me to interfere. In fact, I added, if he took care of it, the fly would probably last forever because my friend claimed his flies were virtually indestructible.

"You don't say!" Then it was the fisherman's turn to laugh. "I was here Sunday night—parked in that very spot. I found the fly in my driveway Monday morning. It was stuck to my front tire. Indestructible! Why hell, I drove the forty miles to Butte with it imbedded in my Goodyear, and it's still catching fish!"

Dumbfounded, I then introduced him to the one and the only: McDuff's Knutt. When he wondered out loud, "Why McDuff's Knutt?" I just told him it was a long story, no sense wasting any more good fishing time. Besides, the whole scene was too weird. It was kind of like seeing someone date your ex-girlfriend. After exchanging final pleasantries, I turned to climb up the high bank leading back to the gravel road where my rig was parked.

When I reached the plateau there was a splash, and then several more. Looking down upon the river, another fine rainbow was tail dancing across the water, dangling in midair off the indefatigable McDuff's Knutt. When the angler finally landed the sixteen-incher, he turned and looked up in my direction. "Sure wish I could keep him!"

"Don't even think about it," I shouted.

As he released the fish, I realized that Jerry had indeed created a monster.

Gramps

Autumn in the Northwest can be a season of fleeting beauty. Golden yellows accented by a splash of red saturate the senses in a tapestry of colors framed by the verdant backdrop of coniferous forests. In British Columbia, this can all end, and usually does, with an early blast of winter or, at the very least, a cold rain accompanied by a sobering, bitter wind.

This year we were lucky. "Indian Summer" lasted for several weeks. On the other hand, we were not so lucky with regard to fishing. Since steelhead prefer miserable weather, they had been slow to arrive. Nonetheless, it was about the time that these legendary creatures were just starting to rise to the fly when the sad word arrived from New York that Grandma had finally passed on to a better place.

At least, that's the way she would have viewed it. Imprisoned by senility, my grandmother's more lucid moments were filled with the repeated utterance, "It sure is terrible to grow old." What she didn't question was the cosmic unfairness that caused her to spend many of the final and supposed Golden Years of life incapacitated, drifting in and out of the scattered memories of events and experiences that, piece by piece, formed her ninety-eight years of existence. In the end, she just sat impatiently, as if waiting for a train that would take her home.

I have never believed that life is a series of random events haphazardly strewn together by the forces of chance and luck. Sure, that is a part of the total picture, but we are also the sum total of our choices intertwined with the influences of those people—good or bad—who have touched our existence since birth. Throw in some unexplainable events, hardships, and improbable coincidences, and that's life. Ultimately, it is how we choose to deal with all these factors that make us who we are. And if we believe in a unifying Force that ties this whole package together, the subjective meaning of life can expand into a dimension of unlimited proportions.

Grandma was always pleased when she knew my brother Rick and I were off fishing somewhere together. This year's great rendezvous found us both on the Bulkley River in search of the ultimate steelhead experience. She probably never realized that if it weren't for her and Grandpa, neither of us would have been in northwestern Canada on the day when she passed away. If it weren't for my grandparents, this zest for fishing would have never been cultivated at an impressionable age, nor would that enthusiasm have been passed on to my younger brother. Because they did what good grandparents should do, the only roads worth traveling in later life were the ones that led to a river. The meaning of life became synonymous with the number of days spent with a fly rod in hand.

Reflecting upon her death, I realized the last piece in an intricate chain of life's determinates was now immortalized. Fittingly, it had only been a few months earlier that a chance encounter with two inveterate fly fishermen on Idaho's Henry's Fork of the Snake River rekindled an appreciation for my long-departed Grandfather, and the impact his life had upon my being in that precise place many years after his death.

While searching for just *one more fish*, I met Tom and Tim entrenched in deep conversation as they gazed over the Bonefish Flats section of Henry's Fork from a grassy bank. Despite the crowd, the day already had been a productive one thanks to the Pale Morning Dun. After chatting with the two friends, it was apparent they had a relationship with "the Fork" that spanned decades. About then, Tim proudly revealed that on this very day, he was celebrating his thirtieth anniversary fishing this legendary water on a yearly basis. The two fishing buddies had stuck with the river through the good times and the bad, and this obvious bond connecting everything in their lives, past to present, emanated a profound enthusiasm that had not dimmed with time. The two frankly discussed the changes on the river in recent years without the least bit of pessimism, and they both agreed that the greatest alteration in the demeanor of Henry's Fork was the attitude of the present-day angler.

"With today's equipment," Tom commented, "and a week's worth of lessons, these modern-day purveyors of the sport can cast better than I ever will. But what is lacking is passion, and the zeal to understand the world of trout and how to relate to them in a broader sense. All they want to do is catch lots of fish. It's a sign of the times; people are looking for the quick fix these days."

The two went their own way, quietly blending into the gathering. Two beings of substance lost in the faceless sea of modern fly fishing. Lost also is the link to the traditions of the sport as the "Toms and Tims" subtly give way to the irreverent new shoot-from-the-hip approach to the rivers. "Fly fishing used to be a religious experience," a friend recently quipped. "Now it seems like an atheistic one."

Unlike baseball, or even golf, two sports dedicated to their colorful pasts, this steadily unfolding attraction of casting a fly seems too self-indulgent at present to honor and respect the traditionalists. Fad, fashion, and greed threaten to dilute the forces that called many of us to the rivers long before it was the "in thing." Sure there are Wulff, Bailey, Haig-Brown, et al., but the existence of many other solitary apostles appear destined to fade long before the refined expression of this art form is ever recognized. These days, only a dreamer would expect anything more. For those who understand the distinction, keeping that thread tied to the past before it completely unravels takes on a desperate urgency. Remembering our mentors with respect—the brother, uncle, father, grandfather or the anonymous devotee encountered on an obscure section of forgotten waters—may be the only hope of keeping this spirit alive. Tim's thirty-year loyalty to Henry's Fork will go unnoticed by most, but such commitment is a heroic achievement that should be appreciated by everyone who ever picks up a fly rod.

I don't have many heroes, nor have I read extensively everything written on the sport of fly fishing. It was, however, the works of Joe Brooks and his drive to catch a trout just about anywhere they swam that peaked my attention in the early seventies. The Yellowstone cutthroat on page thirty-nine of *Trout Fishing* left an impression inspiring the changes that eventually led down the path of many great trout experiences. I longed to relive some of Joe's adventures and in many small ways, I have tried, but there still remain unfulfilled dreams and the sad reality that many of his footsteps can never be followed again. Too many things have changed too quickly; in a short period of time the world has been tamed. The paths beaten along the rivers and the boats filling them serve only as poignant reminders of vanishing solitude and lost secrets. Only through the written word can the spirit of the pioneer fly fisherman now be experienced, captured in stories that in all probability are bigger than life itself. After all, isn't that what heroes are all about?

I learned to fly fish many years before I ever saw a fly rod. It all started with an appreciation of a great river, the Niagara, when I grew up in the close vicinity of its polluted shoreline. To some, fishing becomes more than just the linear event of catching a fish. It evolves into a lifestyle, a state of mind that expresses life in the most simple of terms. Fly fishing becomes the quintessential form of this statement when one's being becomes intertwined with this pursuit and its many related creative expressions. The catalog in the mail the other day boasted that its school could teach fly fishing in just three days. There is no doubt these instructors can teach folks how to cast and even catch some fish in a matter of three days, but there is a catastrophic leap of commitment between catching a fish on a fly rod and fly fishing. Understanding the difference can take a lifetime. Starting with a can of worms on the Niagara over forty years ago, my involvement with fly fishing began.

Long before Joe Brooks, there was the influence of another great fisherman who believed in the tradition that fishing was the reward of an honest day's work. This man was my grandfather; we affectionately called him "Gramps." In an age of Captain Midnight and Mickey Mantle, an eight-year-old boy knew a hero when he saw one. Gramps could catch a fish anytime, anywhere, of that I was convinced. I watched him crank in black bass, rock bass, and yellow perch off the cement dock that jutted into the Niagara near our home when everyone else was catching only shiners and stonerollers. Every now and then, on Saturday mornings, he would get up at the crack of dawn, and by ten o'clock Gramps would return from "the dock" with a bucket full of yellow bullheads. These whiskered oddities were big, and we never knew of anyone *ever* to catch one off the dock, except for Gramps. Normally, the only bullheads we saw were floating dead. I always wondered just how he knew those live ones would be there on Saturday mornings.

Gramps was gruff and, at times, grumpy. His brusque demeanor reflected a stoic Germanic upbringing, and without saying a word, his intimidating presence would keep us grandchildren on the straight and narrow. But through this hardened exterior, we could sense a caring man. Kids know about such things. And when it came to fishing, he would have laughed at the thought of catching a fish on a fly. It was only red garden worms for him, and to hear Gramps tell it, he grew the best worms on the planet in the manure pile next to his backyard garden. Of course, he imported the highest-quality manure on the continent from the farm just around the corner—at least, according to him. Immediately before a summer evening outing at "the dock," Gramps would dig while my cousin Paul and I picked the juiciest of squirmy morsels out of the pungent pile of aging poop, tossing back those deemed unworthy by his watchful eye. Into the old Maxwell House coffee can they would go, and when we had enough for the evening, he topped them with a dusting of manure. After the holes were poked into the homemade lid (an ironic act of mercy considering we were about to impale the contents and toss them to their watery doom), we all headed to "the River." Grandma came along to watch "the boys" because if one of us happened to fall in, it was doubtful that Gramps would have ever noticed. Once the fishing began, he didn't like to be bothered by anything.

We learned quickly to tie on the homemade lead sinkers and to bait our snelled hooks with the garden worm offerings, for it took only a few grumbles from where Gramps was sitting before we realized we were on our own. The level wind reels of those days presented many problems to young boys, especially when they "backlashed," leaving an explosion of line on the reel known to us as a "bird's nest." Gramps would patiently allow about one mishap per night, but when his mumbles turned to stern utterings that sounded like "son-of-a-pup," we knew to stay clear, though it wasn't exactly clear what he meant. Grandma's contribution was meek, and it went something like, "Don't get too near the water, boys." But since getting near the water was an essential ingredient to our main objective, we both would obediently shift backwards only about an inch.

Paul and I loved to fish. Since our ages were about the same, and since we lived next door to each other, we habitually searched the fields behind our houses together and explored the River at the end of the country road like a fifties version of Huck Finn and Tom Sawyer. In the process, we steadily learned the ways of the dock. Our understanding of nature grew as we did. We found that the rock bass lived next to the rotted old pilings, the perch swam the edges of the weed beds, and the sheepshead (freshwater drum) were a good cast into the rock-filled mudflat off the left-hand side. Eventually we caught fish, but we were never too young to notice the beauty of the setting sun as it descended upon Canada on the opposite shore like a giant orange ball. The smell of the humid air mixing with the interesting scent of the river in the coolness of a darkening summer evening still lingers in the olfactory memory of my mind. And as the crickets chirped while the last boat disappeared over the glass smooth surface of the Niagara, we would hear the train. There was always a train that echoed through Canada, enchantingly touching our imaginations. Though we could never see it, as hard as we tried, looking for that phantom became an integral part of our youthful fishing adventures.

As we grew older, Paul and I weaned ourselves from the vigilance of Grandma and the grumblings of Gramps. Even so, Gramps's manure pile continued to arm our endeavors as endless hours were spent discovering the secrets of the River. We would gladly catch anything that would bite, from the occasional black bass to the lowly sucker. Most of our quarry would be comprised of small rough fish like shiners and chubs, and we learned the value of catch-and-release soon enough when Paul's dad found a forgotten carp stinking up the garage on a humid August evening.

Paul became quite the angler. Once he hooked seventeen bass on eighteen casts, and when he lost that huge muskellunge on a novelty lure from his father's collection, we knew our fishing adventures had climbed to a new plateau. Paul's father was a liquor distributor and, as a promotional gimmick, he handed out treble-hooked fishing spoons with the name of some whiskey painted on the gold peened surface. We never thought they would be worth a darn for actual fishing, but that fish proved us wrong as it jumped through our lives for years. Although we rarely went fishing with Gramps ever again, he was always interested in our stories. To our amazement, Gramps still continued to catch yellow bullheads on Saturday mornings.

The older we got, the more Paul and I visited the River separately. About this time the naive world of our youth was shattered by the growing awareness of poisoned waters. I learned to ponder the whys and wherefores of life sitting on the shore of the Niagara. Hours of fishing time were also spent looking for a glimpse of that train in Canada, as if seeing the steel rider could magically make all the problems of growing up, including my dying fish, just disappear. I could see the River from my upstairs bedroom window, and on nights of dense air and heavy rain that diesel engine would blow its whistle and rumble seemingly through the backyard. Still, it never came into view, not even its lights.

Gramps passed away several years after I took a teaching job in Utah. It was not a sad event, just an inevitable continuation of life's process. Grandma lived the life of the all-too-common widow until she started to fade in the late eighties. Not long after Gramps's death, the wanderings of Joe Brooks spurred a wonderful life journey that started with a search for the Dolly Varden (just like the one on page forty-five of *Trout Fishing*) before it was reclassified, and then officially renamed bull trout. This obsession took me first to Butte, Montana. It was there, while displaying the long hair and beard requisite for the times, I was urged to continue on to the panhandle of northern Idaho where I was assured that I would find the Dolly Varden for which my heart yearned. Miners, cowboys, and longhairs—songs were written about that combination in those days. And since I didn't feel like becoming a verse in another Hank Williams Jr. rowdy-friends-and-barroom-shit-kicking song, I headed to Idaho.

This strange quest then led to Montana's Bull River, and eventually to the Panhandle's Pack River, where once the famed Dolly Varden did reside. The word was the same everywhere, and it could have been summed up something like, "You should have been here ten years ago, before the river was silted (by errant logging practices) and the fish weren't all pitchforked while they were spawning. Unfortunately, there's not many Dollies anymore." The Pack River produced several anemic ten-inch stocked rainbows and, also, this overwhelming desire to find a bar, slug down some beers, and re-evaluate the direction of this journey. Out of necessity, the nearest rest area was that night's campground, for the good folks of Idaho did not believe in the sight of an empty beer glass. The next morning found me in the dismal little logging town of Priest River looking for the local greasy spoon. This was the end of the line, as close as I could figure, for the Dolly Varden.

It didn't take long before things got a little strange in this little corner of anyplace-but-here. After meeting an ex-Baptist minister at breakfast, then sharing some religious war stories, he introduced me to someone who knew someone else who knew exactly where to find the elusive Dolly. Joe Brooks never indicated that finding one of these critters would be the modern-day equivalent of locating the Holy Grail. There was no choice but to follow this lead. One thing for sure, every last hippie hanging on to any noble cause was stashed quietly away in the crannies of the surrounding mountains, tending to their "crops." Dave the Baptist was right, though; his shirttail friend knew of a few streams north of Priest Lake where we should find DV, and the next day it was "Hello Dolly" time. No one paid attention to the mere technicality that these waters were closed forever to public fishing, a fact discovered in the regulations a few weeks later. Legal eagles they weren't in this neck of the woods. The irreverence for convention that prevailed in this area was appealing, but my belief in the purpose of fishing regulations prevented me from ever fishing illegal waters again.

I made friends quickly. The loggers lived in town, but an assorted variety of outcasts dwelled deep in the hills. Most were long-hairs, and many never showed their faces in public. My Baptist friend told me, "Whatever you do, don't ask about their past." As a rule, I never did. Readily accepted into this reclusive club, I was invited to stay for a while with a married couple who were about my age in exchange for labor on their self-sustaining farm. John and Annie had art degrees from the Rhode Island School of Design, and they put their talents to good use building a funky homestead on the top of an Idaho mountain. John and I hit it off right from the start, since we both grew up in the Buffalo area within the same time frame. It seemed strange to meet someone in the middle of nowhere from a somewhere we both knew well.

Without running water or electricity, there were always chores needing attention. During the evenings John and I would regularly fish Priest River for the odd cutthroat. This was a beautiful piece of water, but the river had been demolished by harsh logging practices for decades. Although fish populations were slim in the area, I was entralled by the freedom of this lifestyle. And though I wanted to head back to Montana, something told me to stay. So I did. After finding the Holy Dolly, it was difficult to leave.

It was only after I had set up residence in a rented cabin that I learned of a unique, but tragic event that happened there decades before. When I contacted my folks to tell them where my recent travels had led, instead of the typical inquiries, a grave silence ripped through the 2500 miles of phone line. Noticeably unsettled, when the words started again, my father told me about his younger brother from Buffalo, New York, who had been killed in Priest River during the early thirties. He was working in the Government's Civilian Conservation Corps program, known affectionately by those from that era as the CCC, and at the age of nineteen he died in a truck that rolled over. It was strange. I knew I had an uncle who died a long time ago, but I never knew the story.

Needless to say, my folks were disturbed. I can't say I wasn't. Some thought it was pure coincidence, others didn't think much about it at all. Jung would call it synchronicity. Whatever it was, I believe unexplainable occurrences happen in life, and when they do, one needs to pay attention to them. At that point, my aimless wanderings seemed to be immediately transformed into a mission. I figured there must be some reason I randomly stopped in the Idaho town that had taken the life of an uncle years before I was ever born. What that mission was has never been exactly clear, or maybe I am living it now without even knowing. Since then, my life has not been the same. But for several years, I stayed in Priest River.

While building a cabin during the following spring on my own five acres of backwoods wilderness, it was then I said my last good-bye to Gramps years after his death. He was a carpenter by trade. I never built a thing. His hands were big and felt like cracked leather gloves; his complexion had weathered to the texture of barnwood. He wore his rugged appearance like a badge honoring all the skills he developed to survive the Great Depression, and it was this versatility that carried him through retirement. He was always banging a nail into something. Guided by his example, and tooled with only a hammer, handsaw, and level, I carried one two-by-four at a time across the creek full of little brookies to that perfect spot on a hill in northern Idaho. There I started to build my little home. As I worked on my roof one beautiful April day, overlooking a forested valley devoid of human life, I felt his presence and heard his words, "You can handle it from here." I could swear he touched my shoulder... and then he was gone.

In the mountains, the wind speaks softly. If there was ever a place to be, this had to be it. Beyond the raw beauty of the region was a realm that occasionally drew me into its bosom. While living alone on that mountain, I thought a lot about everyone who touched my life. I realized then it was the memory of Gramps that motivated and encouraged my new calling as an itinerant fisherman. The role of a hero is to inspire dreams.

A few years later, when Joe's book led me to the upper Big Hole River in search of a grayling, it was there I resolved to fish exclusively with a fly for the rest of my life. Much of what I had already learned provided a solid foundation for this evolutionary progression. Fly fishing in a pure form encompasses so much more than just learning to cast; it has more to do with understanding the fabric that weaves everything together in life. All subsequent rivers and every piece of water explored from that day on had a meaning and a depth that went much beyond catching a fish. And though this journey revealed many other waters suffering from the ignorant transgressions of mankind, I learned from every condition, positive and negative, to understand the ways of trout and man through the ardor of this endeavor. I had two men to thank—one I knew, and one I had never met.

Everyone can't be a hero. It is something neither sought after nor desired, just an honor bestowed upon an ordinary person for having an extraordinary effect on others' lives. Some say there are no heroes anymore, but maybe we are just looking in the wrong places. We put a lot of faith in famous, but undeserving, figures such as movie stars and athletes, to enlighten our lives and show us the way, but many of those to whom we look are clueless when it comes to what is really important. True heroes will always be few and far between; that's what makes them special. Will Rogers once stated, "Everyone can't be a hero, 'cause there has to be somebody on the curb to clap when they pass by." The truth is that the works of many day to day heroes often go unnoticed. I applaud my heroes, and vow I shall never forget them.

I often return to the roots of my childhood. It has been over forty-five years since those first days fishing with Gramps on "the dock," yet that very cement structure still stands as a memorial to the wonderful years of my youth. The Niagara is no longer a flowing river of pollution, either. The fish I catch there, now on my fly rod, symbolize a fitting reunion with that significant force I grew up loving. Sitting on the dock, eyes closed, it all comes back—pleasant memories of simple times. Childhood is such an impressionable age, and I was fortunate to have had a very good one. When I visit the River, I am home again.

Perhaps Gramps wasn't a great fisherman, and I suspect he wasn't; he didn't have to be. In the eyes of an eight-year-old he was the Joe Brooks of the Niagara, and that was all that mattered. After all, he sure knew about those bullheads. On the dock, I learned to ponder, I learned to dream and, thanks to Gramps, I learned to fly fish. In school I hated history, but the older I get the more I realize just how much the past influences the present, and understanding that fact makes everything we do a significant act. As the timeless currents of my River pass, the distinction between past and present narrows, and what is important can no longer be measured. Now, when I hear the diesel blow its whistle, I know I will see that phantom train when it is my time to see it. The mystery alone is a source of contentment.

The morning after learning about Grandma, Rick and I both caught our biggest steelhead of the trip within an hour of stepping into B.C.'s renowned Kispiox River. Afterwards, we dedicated each to Grandma's memory. She would have been pleased. I would like to believe that Grandma went to join Gramps that day; it would only seem right. I would also like to believe in a dimension where everything comes together and makes some sort of sense out of life and death.

The older I get the more it seems that every river I fish is a mere fragmentation of one great flowing ribbon of consciousness where the limitations of space and time have no meaning. In the end, I would like to believe that Joe, Gramps and everyone else worthy will be there, sharing this Great River—fishing the shoreline of eternal peace.

Requiem for a Fly Fisherman

Despite the slight chill in the six a.m. stillness, the day promised to be a hot one, typical of August in Montana. It was the rumor of the pending *callibaetis* hatch and visions of cruising rainbows gulping these mini-sailboats that made the four-thirty wake-up call even the least bit bearable. For a night owl like myself, getting up for anything less inspiring would be impossible.

I'd like to fish still water more. At the beginning of every summer, I vow that this will be *the* season filled with more enthusiastic outings to our local lakes and reservoirs, or at least resolve to make more of an effort to explore the many opportunities these flat waters have to offer. The truth is, I am hopelessly endeared to rivers, the movement and rhythmic sounds of water washing rocks, lapping at log jams, and cleansing the mind in mesmerizing aquatic song. And though you really have to like yourself to fish alone, angling on a lake requires another special sort of discipline. The peaceful sameness and quietude this type of fishing demands, and the effort it requires to maneuver into the trout's realm could be overwhelming to some, or just plain boring to those who prefer water with a current.

Historically, my lake experiences generally start with great intentions, but often the fervor is daunted by some cruel quirk of fate. Usually, I end up in the local bakery eating a Danish, guzzling coffee, and feeling quite fortunate that the thirty mile per hour winds didn't capsize my canoe, or leave me and my float tube stranded in some forgotten bay waiting for the calm of evening. Maybe it's the fear of *deja vu*, or just an overall feeling of ineptness that really keeps me off the lakes. When I look at *all that water*, I can then fully appreciate a river's concise simplicity. In truth, I have to question the depth of my conviction to unlock the secrets of still water when most of my ventures are determined by a lake's proximity to a donut shop.

That morning, there were many reasons to drag out of bed chasing after yet another adventure—the least of which was to catch fish, though I was assured that this was a distinct possibility. Glenn, Federico and I cast off the canoe as the sun rose just a few feet above the Madison range. The water lay flat as a crystal sheet, reflecting the orange tinge of the budding dawn. The white pelicans dotted the smooth horizon of Ennis Lake, lords of this watery domain, and the eared grebes scurried about their business like court jesters, bobbing gracefully below the surface to breakfast on the numerous Utah chubs swimming amid the weedy entanglements. We paddled in prayer-like silence, solemnly revering the purpose of this pilgrimage, and pensively reflecting upon Glenn's words as we pulled away from shore: "This one is for Bill."

I met Bill only once, but knew of him through our mutual friend, Glenn. Bill was to be admired for his unconventional approach to life. In a world of conformed competitiveness, his offbeat lifestyle did not configure with the hard drive of modern existence, but this didn't faze Bill. Though I would have really welcomed the opportunity to get to know this free-spirited character, I now realize we were kindred souls that had often touched in the timeless dimensions of the rivers we shared. To partake in this requiem with two who had known him well was indeed a meaningful honor, and a fitting tribute to a man who quietly loved the sport of fly fishing and died in the devoted pursuit of it.

Nineteen ninety-one was not a good year for angling greats. With the passing of Lee Wulff, Robert Traver a.k.a John Voelker, and A.J. McClane, the void created looms even greater in an era of hi-tech, bottom-line, big-business fly fishing. These men will be immortalized for their many distinguished accomplishments

and contributions to the sport. From the ingeniously creative and whimsically philosophical to the educationally informative, these legends will live on in the waters we fish, wraiths of the warm summer breezes that lift the evening hatch gently off the surface to its inevitable destiny.

In fly fishing, because of its inherent solitude and traditional noncompetitive nature, there is no simple gauge to determine one's impact on the sport. There are no box scores, no Oscars, no winners or losers, just degrees of devotion—and, fortunately, this can't be measured. For every legend, there are many others who contribute with contemplative significance a lifetime of dedication, leaving behind a spirit comingled with the greats and shared by those of us who care to tune in to their ubiquitous presence midst the lakes, rivers, and streams we frequent. It is not the size of the fish or the number caught, but the depth and the love of the experience that is a true measure of one's legacy. Though subjective, in the end this is all that really matters.

Bill MacAfee was not famous, but he was known, loved, and appreciated by many for his enthusiasm, understanding, and spirit of adventure. He was a gentle man, and a gentleman. Bill approached fly fishing with meticulous deliberation, as he did life itself. The ability to stop, look, and truly see all that surrounds one has become a lost art, but Bill was its Master. As a guide from Argentina to Alaska, many of his clients learned that to fish with him was less a matter of catching fish than it was a total fishing experience or, better still, a life experience. Though fame was not the least bit important to Bill, his commitment to the sport of angling with a fly was in itself noteworthy. His premature passing stole from all of us his unique presence. Besides, there were still too many rivers left to fish.

Glenn Brackett, the bamboo guru at the Winston Rod Company, shared many remarkable adventures with Bill, bonding both of them together in years of noble friendship. From the southern tip of South America to the Arctic extremes, they had wandered. Glenn, whose reflective involvement with life is mirrored by his mild demeanor and the exquisite artistic expression of his craft, knew that Bill would take great delight in this day's ceremonious endeavor.

Federico Prato, a young and handsome Argentine bamboo artisan, guided with Bill for several years. Some say there was a notable similarity in the way they both perceived life. This trip to the States had to be especially difficult for Federico. A planned stop on his journey would have been to visit Bill, but the word came shortly after his arrival that Bill's plane had crashed in the Alaskan bush country, the summer of 1991.

The canoe continued to glide silently over the slick surface, dragging from time to time on a bed of weeds. The *callibaetis* were already beginning to emerge. Once one has developed an appetite for taking trout on a dry fly, this quest becomes somewhat narrowed at particular times of the year. In the past, August represented the long, hot, dry season responsible for the sluggish aquatic life found in rivers often devoid of water. This sense of dormancy seemed nature's inconvenient advent to September, the month of fall's splendor in the northern Rockies, as well as the resurrection of Montana's splendid fishing. But over the years, I have also learned to take advantage of August's subtle treasures. Morning tricos, some afternoon hoppers, and the occasional mousing brown at night all shed a new enthusiasm for the month that houses the "dog days" of summer. Add chasing the *callibaetis* hatch to the list, and the once misunderstood August now can be downright delightful—even if it does mean risking a windy day or two.

By the time we reached the inlet where one of several braided channels of the Madison River enters the lake, the *callibaetis* were twittering the surface. Many nice-size, creamy-tan mayflies were laying flat on the surface film, wings outstretched and vibrating the tiniest of ripples. Others sat motionless, wings upright, drying in the warm summer morning air. Perched on the shore, we

watched for the first fish to show in a rather broad area of the
shallow lake, broken by an island, and dotted by hundreds of the
mayflies commonly referred to only by the Latin nomenclature
of its genus.

I didn't dare sour the mood, but in my mind I figured it was
just a matter of time before the wind began to blow. The wind
sure can blow on Ennis Lake and, normally, it does. Just as likely,
the sun would certainly become so bright and hot that this
magnificent hatch would continue its life cycle while the trout
searched for shade out of the warm shallows. Predisposed to
the fickle nature of lakes from past experiences, I continued to
consider all the negative possibilities. Then it happened—
significant, but not dramatic. From the south, a sky full of high
clouds began to block the rising sun as if someone hung a
wispy gray curtain from the highest point of blue. The day
remained still.

Alone on the lake's south shore, the three of us sat suspended
in trancelike concentration, glaring at the water as if it were a
mantra for all the truths of life yet to be revealed; and, indeed,
several truths became evident. One by one, noses attached to
feeding mouths began to appear, and it was a thing of beauty.
Glenn began to stalk the shoreline, and I paddled Ferderico across
the channel, where he proceeded on his search. The serene
grayness of the day's aura merged our beings in a meaningful
oneness. I pointed the canoe out toward a pod of noses, and
slowly cruised in that direction.

I heard a splash before getting close to my destination, Federico
was fighting a rainbow that glittered despite the dull light. After a
few minutes, the weeds and, ultimately, the fish won the first
encounter. I continued and found that anything less than a low
profile approach to these fish from the canoe would be a fruitless
effort. I spooked the first pod without much effort at all.

As Glenn and Federico got smaller, I was still able to hear
their voices and see the splashes. I had a choice of several feeding

pods, but putting a sneak on them in the calm, clear water only a few feet in depth was a challenge. My tactic was simple. Slide with slow deliberation toward the fish, take one last quiet stroke with the paddle, pick up my rod, and then make a perfect cast. After several not-so-perfect casts, it all came together. Finally a long, decent presentation landed the fly gently in the vicinity of four gulpers. My fur and feather imposter just sat there on the glass-smooth surface. Then, progressively, a very nice rainbow worked itself toward my offering, slurping up *callibaetis* at one-foot intervals along the way. Slowly, inch by inch, the fish made its way to my fly, and with one final, carefully calculated look, it decisively "gulped" the parachute imitation. The fish reacted immediately. In fast-forward, the silver bullet zipped out all the fly line as the reel sang well into its backing. A bit of pressure and the fish was towing the canoe toward a huge wall of weeds. Naturally the weeds won again, but at that point I knew I was on to something.

While still retrieving the limp length of line, a major splash resounded across the placid silence. Turning, I could tell, despite the distance, that Glenn had hooked a fine fish. The leaping dynamo resembled an exuberant steelhead. It also exhibited all the characteristics of the mythical "big one" that always gets away. Given the status of the weed situation, it would seem this fish should be home free in a matter of seconds—the makings of another great fish story. Knowing that Glenn would fill me in on the details when we convened later, I refocused.

Sitting without movement, another pod fed well within reach of my canoe. Casting once again, I hooked, fought, and released a fairly chunky brown trout. Infrequently encountered in the lake, this trout's fight was strong. And though it lacked the zesty gusto that defined the lake-dwelling rainbows living in the same water, I quickly dismissed any hint of disappointment that this was *just* a brown trout and not one of the feisty bows that seemed to be teaching us all a lesson this day. In fact, I felt fortunate to finally get a fish to the net.

Glancing toward Glenn, amazingly, he was still entwined in the same weed-filled battle with the Goliath of Ennis Lake. It appeared that just as he would free the fish from one mass of weeds, it would dart to another, and so on the battle went. Maybe it was out of sheer frustration that the fish gave up, or maybe it sensed powers too great to overcome. But finally, Glenn slowly backed toward shore. Holding the doubled-over bamboo rod high above his head, he patiently worked the big fish toward him. Finally under control at his feet, Glenn bent over and gently removed the fly from the hefty rainbow's mouth. In a matter of seconds, it scooted away. Then Glenn got out of the water, walked over to the most comfortable patch of grass he could find, and sat. The death of his best friend was not easy to accept. And though Bill was gone, I am sure Glenn resolved that Bill would remain forever present in the world he left behind. After tangling with a few more nice fish, I picked him up two hours later. He was asleep when I approached.

The flies were still hatching, and the fish were still rising. We could have fished until dark. But on that day, it would have been pointless. Glenn's eyes told the story, and without saying a word, it was obvious we had just shared something very special. Finally I asked, "How big was that fish?"

"Oh, it was big!" Glenn's voice was reflective, but his mind was distant. I then realized that this was about as much detail as I'd ever get out of him about its size or its significance.

We climbed into the canoe and paddled over to Federico's side of the channel. Federico, a man of few words, summed it up best. Giving us his characteristic OK sign, displaying forefinger and thumb together in a ring, he poetically uttered one word in unbroken, easy-to-understand English: "Perfect!"

The way back to the landing was a pleasant blend of fulfilled contentment and small talk. A final chapter had been written for Glenn and Federico, and it was a fitting one. Once on shore, Glenn pronounced with conviction, "Well, I guess Bill smiled on us today!"

About the only thing lacking that day was a lone hawk soaring above us in the ethereal thermals of Montana's big sky. Of course, our eyes were so transfixed upon the water, we never looked up. I'm sure it was there.

We loaded our gear.

Silence prevailed.

Upon our departure, we took one last glance at the lake from the bluff. It was at peace.

So were we.

The Big Mack Truck Attack

When summer finally arrives in the mountains of central Idaho, the air gets thick and still while the scent of pine and cedar hang heavy in the silent forests too warm for the slightest stir of any life. The fly angler awaits the evening shadows at times like this, and the hundred mile drive to Rock Creek would deliver me there at about the right time. As the road to Montana passes hypnotically beneath the front tires, the lull of sweeping curves and magnificent scenery is as comforting to a weary soul as a pillow. It was just a brief nod of the head. You know the feeling, when the eyelids get so heavy and sleep beckons like a soothing mythical Siren from the depths of your being. Ah, just for a short restful second...it feels so good!

At that moment, my eyes popped open in a frightening instant, resisting this enchantingly dangerous lure with every mortal fiber of my body. While fear has the ability to wake the senses in a split second, reality lags behind in a lifetime of moments; certainly the eighteen-wheeler locked dead-on course to gobble up my small Datsun pickup was but a dream—and a real bad one at that. Wasn't it?

But when a flash of alertness confirmed that this wasn't a dream, the decision about what to do had to be conceived and solved in about one second. Instinct? Maybe! Guardian angel? Who knows! The resolution to cut across the steadfast behemoth's path as it came upon me like a dragon from hell and bail into the ditch on the opposite side of Montana's twisting Highway 12 just happened. Once there, the tires caught the shoulder; brakes, dust, and then flight. Over once, twice, a third time, and possibly a fourth. I've heard of "out-of-body" experiences before, and maybe this was one. It was as if the whole macabre event was projected on a big screen TV, and the stuntman looked just like me. But when the old Datsun came to rest on what was left of its tires, I sure enough was sitting behind the wheel.

Wow! The windshield was gone, the roof was crushed, and I think I was still alive. The Loggins and Messena tape in the deck continued its lively repertoire as if nothing had happened. Amidst the glass and grit, it dawned on me, "Damn! No fishing this weekend." I then thought about my uncle who was killed in a truck rollover during the thirites in northern Idaho. It was eerie. I crawled out, dusted off, and except for a few scrapes and bumps, I truly had survived. But lying there next to my barely recognizable rig (as we call our vehicles in the West) was my eight and a half foot Fenwick that hadn't been quite so lucky, and that confirmed it. I just sat and contemplated existence.

It's funny how life evolves. Working for the Forest Service in Idaho's Selway-Bitterroot wilderness during the seventies in a less-than-stimulating position was really nothing to complain about. I had often counted my blessings for having the insight to abandon the temptations of the city several years beforehand to find refuge in the mountains. Most folks only dream of doing the same thing. My schedule was pretty straight forward. I got off work daily at three thirty and was fishing on my "home river," the Lochsa, or one of its tributaries by three forty-five. Every Friday, I hopped into the pickup at three-thirty and headed for

Rock Creek, or any other Montana river I could get to and return from by midnight Sunday. Not that Montana had more to offer than Idaho, there just seemed to be an inexplicable force that repeatedly summoned, as if the source of all that made sense somehow flowed through its rivers.

The only glitch in this schedule would be those damnable forest fires that occasionally occurred during seasonal dry periods. For some reason, these blazing infernos seemed to get the blood boiling in every loyal government worker I knew. Overtime and hazard pay added up quickly. Other than that, it was tough to figure the attraction. The work was grueling and forest fires rarely happen in cool, comfortable weather. You eat smoke, and afterwards blow black mucus out your nostrils for weeks. Hats off to those loyal to this line of work. There's no tougher job, and after a few attempts, I found it was not for me. Mandatory weekend fire duty was hard to avoid, but with some inside help, I was able to maneuver out of Idaho when needed on Fridays under some sort of contrived ruse. Fire or fish—it didn't seem like much of a choice.

There was something missing though. I wasn't bored, just unfulfilled; not with fishing, just with all the time that filled in between. I could never get tired of the herbal-scented Lochsa River, the comforting silence, and the most exquisite westslope cutthroats one could imagine. From the deep pools of emerald, these red-cheeked, sparsely spotted beauties would deliberately rise to almost anything floating on the crystal-clear surface. Although they would often intercept even the most inept presentation of artificial temptations, that suited me just fine. There was something about these fish that was pure magic. The total experience was an ever-changing watercolor, many dimensions of sight and sound displayed in a poetic motion that made the rest of hum-drumness even more pronounced. The time for change was imminent. I was just looking for a sign.

Staring at my crumpled Datsun, I knew I had found one.

Simplicity's virtue lies in its lack of complexity; and life, as I knew it, was pretty simple. In fact, everything I owned fit into my pickup. Living under a camper shell was the epitome of getting back to basics. After fishing during every conceivable moment of the day, just flopping into the back of the truck at dark wherever the last cast took place was about as convenient as it could get.

At that moment, however, my life was inconveniently lying shattered in the ditch. When word of the mishap got back to the ranger station, a contingent, led by my supervisors, kindly assisted in the rescue mission. I wasn't up for much small talk; neither was the highway patrolman on the scene. He did have mercy on me, though, and wrote no citation. Upon departing, he unofficially mumbled that this had been a particularly rough day on Highway 12, for mine was the seventh accident. Seven may be a lucky number for some, but for me, it all depended on how you looked at it.

It didn't take long to pick up my life. Gathering what was left of my scant belongings, along with the memories, and throwing them into the back of someone else's pickup was a sad testimonial to the tenuous nature of existence. The ride with my boss back to the ranger station where my cat and small government trailer awaited reminded me that it would be a long weekend in July without a vehicle. But the forecasted heat boded well for the traveling cat. In that kind of swelter, it was best to leave her in a neighbor's care for a few days; she lucked out. Overwhelmed by loss, the cat was a comfort. To make matters worse, I knew things would be hopping later that evening on Rock Creek. Once the big-time salmon fly and golden stone hatches had passed, a solace would subtly envelop this beautiful piece of water as everyone moved on to other things. Ironically, there wouldn't be a better place to be than Rock Creek at a time like this.

The fact that hardly a muscle moved the next morning tempered my disappointment, for just getting out of bed to scrape together a breakfast was a worthy accomplishment. By now, the reality of the previous day had set in. The concept of "borrowed time" echoed through a sore head. The struggle to stay awake at the wheel had fallen exactly one half mile short from a designed plan to pull over at a rest area along Lolo Creek to catch a snooze. The previous long, but rare night of discussing world problems while peering into the bottom of a beer glass had gotten the best of me. Damn! Just another minute, and I would have made it to my destination.

Sulking around the compound while licking my wounds that Saturday was made much easier by all the kindly attention from concerned co-workers, many of whom I barely knew. The thought of sitting quietly on a log under the shade of some old pine sounded like a comforting activity for the day. After the invitation came my way to attend a mid-July picnic, it was with much reticence, but I politely accepted. Social smoozing was not in my character, but I guessed this was the kind of thing most folks who don't fish do on weekends.

With a formal philosophy background interwoven between sundry other science courses and tied neatly together into a diploma lost en route between somewheres and plenty of nowheres, I pretty much had things figured out by my mid-thirties, or so I thought. Life, and fishing as an integral part thereof, was always something I endlessly contemplated. Based on living the statistical average life expectancy, maybe I had five hundred months remaining, give or take a few. With only thirty-five, maybe forty Julys left, the thought of blowing even one of those weekends not fishing was discomforting. As I saw it, everything important somehow boiled down to making the most of every last finite month, week, day, and minute available. My brush with mortality only emphasized these calculations. I undoubtedly walked away with a heightened appreciation for life, as well. Though the accident certainly led to a deeper degree of reflection on life's meaning from a much different perspective, fly fishing still figured prominently. As my body twitched with pain and my being ached for Montana, I felt as antsy as a caged cat in a roomful of mice. Though I had never spent a summer weekend at the ranger station before, I have always believed in the forces that bring significant elements together for an ultimate purpose. Every event has meaning, while each possesses the powerful potential to change the course of time. For lack of a better explanation, this belief consoled my state of bewilderment.

When she approached, I didn't think much of it. The beer flowed freely (no one had to drive anywhere), and the volume of hot dogs sizzling on the grill could have filled a logging truck. Volleyball was the game of choice by those who had muscles that worked. The Lochsa looked particularly enticing, even on a Saturday; but for me the Lochsa was never a Saturday kind of river. She asked me in a very caring way about the accident, and I provided the startling details to the best of my recollection.

She was a schoolteacher from the West Coast working on the Lewis and Clark trail reclamation project as a part of her master's thesis. Her name was Debra. Most single ladies working for the USDA at the Powell Ranger District were always too youthful; and besides, this was the year I had already decided to take a sabbatical from the relationship scene. At the risk of sounding politically incorrect, it always puzzled me why the faction of the female population I always met seemed to prefer men of questionable character traits over the quiet, somewhat thoughtful type of male. Maybe it was just the way things were back then. My opinions were obviously slightly skewed from a misdirection or two over the previous few years. As I see it, some women interpret brash, arrogant cockiness as synonymous with confidence, an illusion many inadequate men are well adept at selling. On the other hand, the so-called "nice guy" is often described in sentences ending with boring or wimp. It could be that the nice guy never wins because, for him, winning is not worth the deceptions. So much for common sense, and the idle rantings of a self-proclaimed nice guy. In the *yin* and *yang* of existence, fishing a lot seemed like fair compensation. Despite a noticeable degree of aloofness on my part, Debra seemed interested in me. My firm resolve for temporary, self-imposed celibacy was wavering.

With no word from the "good hands" insurance people the following week, the prospect of another Montana-less weekend became more and more likely as each day passed much too quickly. When senior engineer John Sipe handed me the keys to his 1971 1300cc Datsun pickup with attached camper on Friday morning, my spirit was resurrected. John knew the value of weekends away from the high country, and he understood the need to pursue a dream. For years he would regularly head up to Flathead Lake to build his "dream house," utilizing every weekend he could possibly squeeze into a summer season. He was about a year away from early retirement, and the promise of spending the rest of his life on the lake fueled his thoughts. Additionally, that very topic filled most of our conversations. He knew also that my gratitude for his unsolicited gesture of kindness was genuine; at least I told him so. When he died of cancer two years later at his Flathead home, John got to fulfill his dream much sooner than he expected.

At exactly three forty-five that afternoon, I was headed out toward Montana with a borrowed rig, a backup flyrod, rekindled enthusiasm, and eyes that were wide awake. I barely turned onto the highway of doom when I saw her standing there hitching a ride to Missoula. I guess some things are just meant to be. I pulled over, picked up Debra, and off we chugged in John's old beater of a pickup. We had plenty of time to discuss events of the week while slowly puttering up the pass. Fortunately, we ran out of pass before we ran out of power as the Datsun, with a sewing machine for an engine, did its best imitation of "the little engine that thought it could." Once at the top, it was all downhill to Missoula, and then Rock Creek.

The time it took to drive into town dissolved in a blink; our discussion continued to flow from the soul. It did seem unusual for two people pushing their mid-thirties to have never been married and to have had no children. We shared the belief that it was better to lead a productive single life than to succumb to the all-too-common status quo marriage with 2.3 children and a fifty percent divorce rate. At one point, I'm sure we both had thought about raising a family—images drilled into us from childhood. But if that didn't happen, so be it. Forcing the situation for all the wrong reasons causes numerous problems, particularly for the children. We were neither desperate to stay single nor in a hurry to get married. More importantly, we were comfortable with our independence. It seemed obvious to us that the curious circumstances leading to our chance encounter needed further investigation. When I mentioned that it was too bad we couldn't have planned a weekend camping trip together on Rock Creek, Debra solved that problem immediately. Without hesitation, she purchased a sleeping bag at a Missoula sporting good shop, and off we went.

As it turned out, Debra only had another two weeks before she returned to the Bay Area to begin the new school year teaching at a private institution. By midweek, the insurance company had covered my regrettable blunder with enough of a settlement to replace the destroyed pickup (only if I added about thirty-six extra payments). Oh well! It just felt good to be back in business. When Debra accepted my invitation to share one last trip together, we cruised over Lolo Pass into Montana the following Friday afternoon in a brand new Datsun king cab—its maiden voyage.

There was always a coolness along Rock Creek, even in the stagnation of an early August hot spell. The scent of pines and firs filled the air, and the overhanging boughs allowing only thin streaks of sunlight created restful shade. The few active fish available in the low, warm waters were hanging close to the willows or hidden in the canyon shadows of early mornings and late evenings. In between, it felt right to sit for awhile instead of fish. We talked for hours.

We awoke Sunday morning to an unusual summer weather pattern for western Montana at that time of year. It brought a day of pleasant rain, flat light and dripping trees. In an attempt to slowly meander back to Idaho we made one last stop, lingering to prolong our dwindling time together. We walked down the train tracks to the point where Rock Creek enters the Clark Fork River from the opposite side and watched as the creek refreshed the weary-looking bigger water with a thirst-quenching drink of clarity straight from a high mountain wilderness. The Clark Fork usually contained copious clumps of green algae during the warm months, a residual leftover from mining practices gone awry earlier in the century. But on that day, the river didn't look too unsightly, and I knew the fish should be stimulated because of the rain. Although Debra showed no real interest in fishing, she loved the places where trout lived. With a book in hand and covered from head to toe in her rain slicker, all she needed was the comfortable log which the river kindly supplied. Because it continued to rain steadily, reading was out of the question. She just watched.

Rock Creek was obscurely visible upstream as some rainbows responded to hoppers on the rain pattered surface of the Clark Fork. Realizing my time with Debra was limited, I fished for a short while. As I turned her way from the middle of the river, she waved through the misty blur of a rainy August day. As I said before, some things *are* just meant to be. But that would be our last summer day together. The following Friday evening, Debra was waving good-bye as her train pulled out of the station in Missoula. The rain once again began to fall.

I continued on to Rock Creek, but things had changed. The silence was empty, and the melody of its water now seemed hauntingly sad and lonely. Lacking was the dimension only the shared reality of love's vision could provide. As the cold nights of fall hastened the arrival of Idaho's early winter season, I realized this was the last time I would ever call the Lochsa River my home.

Some feel that life is a series of random events; others firmly believe that everything happens with a sense of purpose under God's watchful eye. There are still others who like to think all life is predetermined by some supreme puppeteer, and that everyone is merely acting out a script written for them in some supernatural beyond. Everyone believes in something, even if it is in nothing, and those beliefs make us who we are. Trying to figure out these technicalities is the task of philosophy and theology courses. For me, life is like a charm bracelet; the best choices that determine a meaningful existence should be gathered with a theme in mind. When a certain event in the randomness of life's haphazard occurrences coincides with our life theme, no matter how abstract, it should seriously be considered. Regardless of what you believe, if it almost runs you over—like a Mack truck—you better take notice.

Rivers run through life; and life itself flows like a river. The water that briefly touched our beings was the thread that united us. Over the miles we both knew what we wanted; the river of life embraced us. Debra and I got together that winter, and we married in the warmth of the California summer that followed. Come September, we celebrated our union on Rock Creek.

You can see a lot by just looking, and you can miss a lot by not seeing. It is important to tune in and stay focused. Opportunity doesn't always knock, sometimes it whispers. Vision is the result of not closing your mind and heart to all the possibilities.

Then again, vision is a function of keeping your eyes wide open as well. And whatever you do, be sure to keep them glued to the road that lies ahead.

A Matter of Degree

The knock on the door came a little later than usual that morning. From his little wooded hideaway tucked away on the south shore, Charlie would daily walk across snow-covered McGregor Lake to the cabin Debra and I had rented on Highway 2. Charlie's dwelling had been his family's private retreat for decades and, no doubt, this was his most favorite place in all of Montana. The arrangement was cozy and convenient for us, but the detour cut at least forty-five minutes off his fishing each morning; he never complained. Even ice fishing has its devoted zealots—Charlie was one of them. And since fly fishing opportunities are extremely limited in the northern Rockies during the winter, it was Charlie's enthusiasm that would inspire my regular visits to a series of Montana's "frozen ponds" (pardon the ice fishing lingo).

It should be noted that I have no good recollection of this activity from my childhood days. I would occasionally accompany my grandfather to the Niagara River on a cold January morning, and watch him hoist fine-looking yellow perch, one after another, out of a hole chiseled through ten-inch-thick ice. Though my frozen tears signaled the sorry condition of my outer extremities, they never elicited much sympathy. But distraction did help. I remember popping the eyes out of skinny frozen smelt, sticking them on a hook as bait, and then catching more skinny smelt. This was amusing activity for a kid. A yellow perch would have been a trophy for me, but such angling rewards seemed reserved only for the elders. It was the hope of catching one, though, that kept me glued to that chasm of slush throughout the most uncomfortable of times. Good thing too, because Gramps was not about to leave his honey hole just because my "tootsies" were about to snap like twigs.

Perspectives change in latter years. I realize more than anyone that ice fishing is not fly fishing—not even close. But when the Big Sky State transforms itself into the Big Ice State for a good portion of the year, even the most idealistic of us has to shift gears. I suppose if the knees were in a bit better shape, skiing could help pass the many lingering months of winter. Hockey is out, too. As a former goalie, one too many pucks off the noggin taught me to look at ice a bit differently. In a pinch, I learned that sitting one's butt on a bucket and staring into a dark abyss drilled through two feet of frozen water has its merits, if only in sort of a romantic sense. Overlooking a silent, breathtakingly wild land devoid of any comfort can indeed touch the soul—if not the fingers and toes.

No ice house for me either! Those elaborate shanties designed to make ice fishing a "couch potato" experience were only for the rugged outdoor wannabes as far as I was concerned. Those days with my grandfather at least taught me that. But such idealism, it seemed, only masked hidden desires. The topic of conversation among my cold-footed comrades would often turn to designing the perfect portable ice house. The cold has its way of altering reality, especially when observing the tantalizing smoke wafting out of those makeshift homey-looking boxes as the sun slowly sets in the late afternoon, taking with it the last few degrees of warmth. Drilling more holes (no power augers, please!) is the die-hard's method of generating heat, an act which consistently increases the odds for angler success as well. At least according to our way of thinking, the nomadic Eskimo approach to this sport seems to outweigh the constrictions of a stationary dwelling and the many other inconveniences it brings. Surviving the most drastic of climatic conditions ultimately becomes the true challenge of this form of angling.

Ice fishing is a calling kind of like skydiving or bungee jumping, but its dangers are more disguised and not nearly as dramatic. Although falling through the ice is hardly subtle, dehydration and hypothermia can sneak up if one is not careful. But then I once read about a big ice floe that broke off from Lake Erie's shoreline, stranding several anglers and their vehicles, leaving them to drift helplessly on a temporary winter island. That's dramatic! The anglers were airlifted, but many fine four-wheelers are now havens for baitfish at the bottom of the lake. I also recall sitting on Georgetown Lake in a blizzard, snow drifting over all my gear. It was only luck that I wound up on a road about one mile from my parked pickup after trudging through blowing snow for over an hour in a directionless whiteout. Even ice fishing can be an extreme sport at times.

As for the fish: perch, kokanee, burbot and even lake trout provided plenty of challenge and were ample quarry. Out of deep-seated principles, I would not allow myself to intentionally target the trout that would usually chase one of my flies during the thawed period of the year. At least the cold never affected my heart. McGregor Lake is known for its two to four-pound lake trout, affectionately called "Macs" by the local McGregor crowd, but only coincidentally so. In other parts of the country, the residents have tagged these same fish with localized monikers, as well. In New York, they are called "lakers," and in Maine they are known as "togues." The term "Mac" is actually a contracted form of Mackinaw, the commonly acknowledged Great Lake region where the stock originated that was used to plant various northwestern Montana lakes. And though McGregor Lake fish may be small by all lake trout standards, at least they would fit through the hole. On the other hand, the Macs in nearby Flathead Lake were huge. An opening the size of a manhole was sometimes needed to land those deep-water leviathans. Reports of chiseling out a big crater to extricate forty-pound fish wedged tightly within the existing hole were not uncommon in those days. But for some reason, this type of big game ice fishing never did interest me or any of my cohorts.

Over many seasons, several of us, including Charlie, concluded there was actually a calculated science to ice fishing that came from understanding each particular lake we fished. In McGregor Lake, for instance, we would jig our lures through holes drilled close to shore early in the morning, and then we would gradually move out to seventy feet of water by midday. The process would again be reversed until dark. Lure choices were made based on the brightness of the day. Although some might question the innate wisdom of those attracted to ice fishing in the first place, it is this cerebral approach to the sport that actually improves the angler's odds—not unlike many other forms of fishing.

When I opened the door that February fourth, the condensation froze thick upon Charlie's beard, eyebrows, hat, and scarf as he entered our one-room rustic cabin for a cup of coffee. This not only became a daily ritual before heading out to tangle with a McGregor Lake "Mac" for the day, it also allowed the morning to gain a touch more lightness. Charlie was an early riser. The first words out of his frost-covered head were, "It's cold out there today." Charlie was a mild-mannered, straightforward kind of guy never known to stretch the truth even a bit; for a fisherman, this could have been termed a major character flaw. But to say it was "really cold!!" that particular morning would not have tainted Charlie's reputation one bit.

Although the sun was barely peeking over northwestern Montana's mountains as we started our trek across the ice blanket to the part of the lake aptly known as Mackinaw Bay, there was absolutely no heat in the dead-still morning air. We decided to fish deep that morning in a section of the lake known for its bigger fish, thus departing from our normal tactic of fishing close to shore early. Our faltering "luck" from the past few days needed a jump-start, and this, we strategized, demanded a change of approach. Through the stifling cold, the muffled voices from across the lake sounded close enough to carry on a casual conversation. Sound carries well through frigid air. From what we could observe, there was more standing around a huge fire than actual fishing going on, but their frivolous banter kept us amused on the path to our preset destination. The walk that morning took much longer than planned.

This particular day was unusually cold for the northwestern region of Montana. In fact, there were many days over the years that would be spent sloshing through ankle-deep slush, sometimes in driving rainstorms. It would be difficult to assess which set of circumstances was worse. Dealing with wet feet and gloves for eight hours was no fun either. And trying to release fish back into a hole with three inches of water covering the lake was a challenge as well. Taking the path of least resistance, the small lake trout would do their best bonefish imitation, swimming the flats above the ice until they were recaptured by hand and directed back through the hole to the dark waters below.

As we drilled our first holes for the day, the water that came to the surface froze immediately. It probably took a few seconds. No sense exaggerating! The process of getting a lure to drop fifty or so feet to the bottom of the lake was tedious. Finally there, it was customary to continually jig the lure up and down off the bottom. This movement is essential to successful lake trout fishing. But after finally getting down to business, two jigs later my line went limp. Whether it caught on an edge of ice or whether it was just too damn cold, my monofilament snapped at the hole. Charlie used dacron line to prevent the stretching attributed to mono over a long distance. Although his line didn't break, the freezing water impeded the jigging action of his rod as the line would stick to the constantly forming ice, thus preventing any movement. After the slow and painful re-rigging process of my outfit was completed in the sub-zero temperatures, and my replacement lure had reached the bottom once again, it only took a few more minutes before the monofilament snapped another time like a shattered icicle. By then it seemed we had been on the lake's surface for hours, but in reality, it was less than sixty minutes. Our feet were numb, our heads light; but to serious ice fishermen, quitting was the unthinkable sin. Thirty more minutes passed.

I turned to Charlie, "Coffee and a wood stove would go good about now, and we haven't had any bites."

"Must be this darn high pressure! Macs never bite in high pressure," replied Charlie. True to any form of fishing, there is always an excuse—reasonable or otherwise—for getting skunked.

We quietly packed up our gear, for we barely had the energy to say another word. The retreat back to the refuge of the rented cabin provided quality time for some serious reflection. I contemplated along the way that there had to be some winter fly fishing opportunities somewhere for those of us living in a deep freeze. How about the Bahamas or the West Coast? New Zealand or Argentina held some possibilities. Heck, even Lani Waller tapes might vicariously satisfy this yearning. Nine months of winter for three months of fly fishing hardly seemed like a fair tradeoff. Even a driving rainstorm and wet feet would be welcome relief. The cold sucked my energy like a vampire. I felt drugged. Would I ever see my wife, my dog, or my cat again? Visions and a great white light accompanied euphoric resignation. About the time I had reached the transcendental state of bliss that is closely allied to delirium, we found ourselves on the doorstep of the cabin. Debra naturally had kept the home fires ablaze.

Cold is cold, but some cold is even colder; it is all a matter of degree. In the full morning light, we could now clearly read the large thermometer on the porch at the nearby inn. It registered forty degrees below zero at eleven a.m.

We both sat in front of the fire where we discussed the perfect portable ice house, big Macs that had gotten away in years past, and the beauty of watching a westslope cutthroat slowly rise to the fly on a warm summer day.

"Where do you want to fish this afternoon?" I asked.

"Maybe we should try Mackinaw Bay again," Charlie replied without a waver.

Coffee never tasted better.

A Winter Song

Where the wandering water gushes
From the hills above Glen-Car,
In pools among the rushes
That scarce could bathe a star,
We seek for slumbering trout
And whispering in their ears
Give them unquiet dreams;
Leaning softly out
From ferns that drop their tears
Over the young streams

Come away, O human child!
To the waters and the wild
With a faery, hand in hand,
For the world's more full of weeping than you
          can understand.

From "The Stolen Child"
W.B. Yeats

The snow fell like puffs of cotton. It is a rare day in February when such storms are not accompanied by a northeast blast born in the polar regions of the Arctic. Usually such forces drain into Montana under conditions not fit for any living being, much less a fisherman, and normally it doesn't snow east of the continental divide unless a frigid wind blows hard enough to rip the skin off one's face. Two inches had already fallen, but the portion of the lower Madison River paralleling the two lane flowed in a serenity so alluring that the decision to stop was made without thought. The scene was a subtle blending of grays, browns, and whites, and the dark water passed by like liquid obsidian under the snow-filled sky that draped the surrounding hillside in a blanket of tranquility.

My rod was in the truck. It always is, and the temptation was enticing. This trip was just a business jaunt to Bozeman, and it certainly made good sense to continue the late afternoon, ninety-mile return trip home while the road conditions were still favorable. But the river beckoned with the innocence of a child. I love to fish in the winter, I always have, but it is usually in the form of peering into a black, icy hole on a distant lake with my posterior partially implanted in a five-gallon bucket. And since it is the quest of those who fish to steadfastly seek water, you do what you have to do when you live in a land of perpetual frost. Sometimes, though, the season of cold days and long, colder nights can impart a bonus opportunity to step into surreal splendor, a chance to embrace the gentler side of winter while submerged knee deep in summer memories. So it was, like a child, I proceeded to the river with fly rod in my hand and hope in my heart.

Amidst flashbacks of warm breezes and caddis as thick as the snow that continued to fall, the white fluffs took me to the days of northern Idaho. There, the snow piled high each year in a carpet of silence that would engulf every ounce of consciousness. It defined life down to bare bones. My mind drifted, and I was lost in deep thought until a small rainbow grabbed my nymph and danced like a silver speck on the dark waters of the Madison. Its release was quick—an electric charge that sparked back into the depths until it disappeared like the flake of snow that had just melted as it landed on my reel. For the next hour I fished without thought, but instead, I was entranced in meditation and mesmerized by an aura of white until the mood was breached by the gentle greeting of a bird. Its lively, full-bodied repertoire suspended lightly in the muffled stillness as the rhythms of the passing water accompanied the sweet music of its song.

Usually, it is the charcoal-clad dipper that will come calling at this time of year. This rotund river dweller normally bounces from one rock to another, a delightful entertainer, looking without end under the water and around the boulders for additional morsels to sustain itself until night descends; and then, when the light returns the following morning, it continues the cycle yet another day. But this time it was a dapper-looking gray bird, slender, but fair sized, that sat upon the overhanging bough. It was distinguished by buff-colored wing patches and a white ring encircling each of its bright eyes. Singing once again, the feathered visitor cheerfully faced the elements—alone—in a manner true to its name. The Townsend's solitaire is a relative of the robin, and it lives all year round on juniper-covered foothills throughout the southwestern portions of Montana. This solitary soul was in need of a friend, it seemed, and so we chatted for the remainder of the afternoon.

I continued to drift in and out of thought as an occasional trout and one under-appreciated whitefish interrupted the flow of my subconsciousness. Sometimes I find that catching fish actually gets in the way of fishing. I know this may sound crazy. But for me, it's the anticipation. More likely, it's in "the trying" to catch fish, seeing the rise or feeling the initial take, that often overshadows the inconvenience of actually landing one. The reality is that I just enjoy getting lost in a state of mind without distraction, consumed by the spirit of the land and water as if the total experience affords an ever-so-slight glimpse into the world of eternal bliss.

As the solitaire chirped a few more notes, I was reminded of a recent incident a friend related as we walked the shore of the upper Beaverhead River a few weeks beforehand. Off in the opposite direction, he came across a surly mob of magpies swooping, swatting and pecking at a Townsend's solitaire that seemed curiously tethered to the limb of a willow. Despite being attacked, the helpless appearing bird wasn't going anywhere. In fact, it just hovered above the water like a kite. Upon closer scrutiny, my friend found that the unfortunate creature was indeed attached to the bush by eighteen inches of tippet material. After gingerly gathering the handsome solitaire into his hands, this concerned bird enthusiast noticed that it had tried to eat a #16 bead head pheasant tail nymph which had apparently snapped off on a branch after an errant cast from a passing boat fisherman. Obviously, the luckless bird mistook the dangling fly as a quick snack. Fortunately, the hook was easily removed from the tip of its small beak and the solitaire was safely released to fly once again. My friend showed me the nymph, and we both realized that if he hadn't happened upon it, the bird's fate would have been at the mercy of the magpie marauders. Stretching the concept of catch-and-release to new levels, the episode prompted a discussion about human impact in the form of a size sixteen fly at streamside.

A cheerful chirp refocused my attention back to the Madison. My solitary buddy was still sitting in full view—a rod's length away.

The question of impact has most definitely reached the shores of our favorite waters, and I found myself drifting back to those concerns after a fourteen-inch rainbow made a skillful move to free itself back into its wild world of winter repose. With so many anglers on the rivers these days, it is difficult to assess the true effect of our presence on the resource. For me, this is an uncomfortable issue because my impact is no less than that of any other angler. But then again, I suppose, it is a question of risk and return. On one hand, outdoor resources are regularly compromised to accommodate our passion for just merely being there. But on the other, by virtue of the increased number of avid outdoor enthusiasts, the voice of conservation will have more clout in the future to deal with vital issues which threaten the well-being of these natural havens.

An example which illustrates this point flows close to my home. Over the past several years there have been many of us in southwestern Montana who have worked tirelessly to obtain some public access to the highly-touted Ruby River. Now usually my cynicism is blatantly exposed, a raw canker irritated by any probable threat to our rivers. But I view the public's newfound fortunes with regard to the Ruby as a positive stroke for both the angler and the resource. Naturally, there are some who believe the fishery will be ruined on this portion of the Ruby now that the public has been freely unleashed to "rape, pillage and squander the spoils." While many of us will work diligently to assure that no damage to the fishery is realized from this increase of public pressure, inclusion of the public has renewed the impetus to address some of the broader problems facing the watershed. Public access has been deemed a victory for the resource. Hopefully, all anglers will appreciate the great privilege it is to legally access the Ruby for the first time in years, therefore inspiring the respect this stretch of water deserves. And optimistically, these anglers will all be there the next time the Ruby needs a friend.

Granted, most of the objections with regard to the public gaining access to the Ruby came from new age, wealthy landowners as well as those interested in maintaining a private commercialized fee fishery. Too much fishing pressure from an undeserving public, they believe, will ruin the fishery. And though most of their concerns were self-serving, maybe some issues raised concerning the health of the fish need be considered. I undoubtedly wrestle with something inside myself every time I release another trout. Maybe it is because throughout the West more and more fish bare the scars of abuse and mishandling, likely a few even die, and I have to wonder. Again, it is a fundamental irony. In order to appreciate the beauty of the trout and where it lives, we all subject what we love and cherish to a certain amount of jeopardy.

This is not an unfamiliar paradox. It is even more defined in hunting. After I shot a magnificent elk over twenty years ago, the magnitude of that responsibility led to a soul-searching conclusion inspired by Native American precepts. When the Sioux used to kill bison, they utilized every part of the animal out of honor for its spirit and respect for the land that supported its existence. These people needed the meat to survive, but it was their belief that the slaying of the great buffalo was a sacrifice that could only be justified on a more spiritual level. And despite the fact that not one portion of that elk from my past, hoofs to antlers, was wasted, I decided not to hunt anymore because, for me, the responsibility was too grave. However, since I still catch and then release trout, it has taken much reflection to justify my activity in light of my philosophical position to no longer hunt.

Many have tried to scrutinize the value of angling in this era of "fishing for fun." Some have even questioned its ethics. Since we no longer need to fish for sustenance, does the need to gratify that basic urge to fish justify the price paid by the trout? Well known West Coast steelheader Bill McMillan believes that not even catch-and-release is a good alternative for restoring the depressed wild runs of the Pacific. He proposes total closure, possibly forever on some rivers, as the best way to restore steelhead numbers while respecting the fish at the same time. Although the special circumstances facing West Coast steelhead likely require extreme measures, Bill is among those who dare suggest that anglers find an optional approach to enjoy a river other than through fishing.

It appears this way of thinking is gaining credence to a certain degree. Outdoor philosopher David Quammen fishes less these days while struggling with the implications of catch-and-release. He believes that unless an angler occasionally kills, he may lull himself into believing that he is really not still hunting at the trout's expense—no matter how many fish are released

to swim again. After all, he implies, the game we play is our choice, and not necessarily that of the trout.

Whereas these are noble concepts, there is certainly another side to consider. I have to believe that the trout would, if they could, be willing participants in the games we play, because the salvation of their world is ultimately in the hands of anglers. From the energy of trout, we derive the energy to save them—and the places in which they dwell. This is a burden the trout share together with us. Though not perfect reasoning, it is reality. In the big picture, human impact, not angler impact, poses the greatest threat to their well-being. From cyanide heap leach mining to urban development, these are the "unquiet dreams" of trout, and these continued threats are why their world weeps. Undoubtedly, anglers need to handle trout with respect. Whether we catch-and-release or even kill them, it is through the sacrifice of their freedom that we honor the spirit of trout, as well as the water that supports their existence. From the standpoint of the Sioux, there is no other way to look at it. And as anglers, it would be an empty, somewhat hollow endeavor, if this wasn't our ultimate goal as well.

In Harry Middleton's *The Earth is Enough* old Elias Wonder, the full-blooded Sioux and long time friend of Harry's uncles, once confided to young Harry the basic truth that guided his life. While they fished the Peaceable Kingdom section together on Starlight Creek, Wonder told Harry about a certain custom among his people which he remembered from his youth. As a mark of their approaching manhood, young men would choose a wild creature as badge of character that would stay with them forever. This identity was called a cipher. In a sacred ceremony the young men chose creatures like a fox, a bear or some other symbolic animal to lead them through life. "When my turn arrived," Wonder recalled, "I said loudly, clearly, proudly, 'Trout.' My father smiled and was not ashamed. From that moment on, the trout and I have been inseparable." Thus, for his entire existence, Elias Wonder drew life from trout by giving life to trout. This was the great mystery that sustained him, enriched him...

And just then, the last fish of the day took my fly—a small brown trout. Although it wasn't noticeable while standing in the river, by now there were five inches of snow on the ground. The grayness thickened as the last bits of light squeezed from the encompassing shroud until what remained seemed concentrated only in the reflections of white. The trout that I was about to land punctuated all that I had just considered throughout the afternoon. And in that fleeting moment, while admiring the diminutive brown for all that it symbolized, I said in the process of release, "We all share the burden. Go forth, young trout!"

I then nodded to the Townsend's solitaire in a final salute as I trudged the several hundred yards back to my truck with two inches of annoying hard packed snow clinging to the felt soles of my wading shoes. The song of the solitaire filled my heart with hope. And despite slick roads, in my mind, I fished all the way home.

EPILOGUE

Less than a year later the human child in me had the urge to go fishing in December. Typically, such yearnings go unrequited at this time of year. Since most rivers near my home are usually frozen, options are few. Furthermore, the Madison is usually too far for the couple hours of afternoon fishing a winter day may provide. But in this brief respite from the chiseling gnaw of the Arctic blast that had gripped the state for a good portion of the previous week, the thermometer registered a balmy forty-two degrees. And for the first time in years, I actually had a place to go that didn't require an hour's drive. So it was I sought the slumbering trout. I saw a dipper scurry about. I heard a solitaire's serenade. On that day, there was no one else around. I will continue to yearn for moments like these because, in the spirit of Elias Wonder, the trout and I are inseparable, as well. I am thankful for the opportunity the Ruby River now provides on those rare winter days when a warm breath whispers to those of us who believe in trout—and a whole lot more.

The Caddis Cure

When it comes to flying, I'd rather drive. But then again, I'd rather fish, and flying at least affords more time on the water—a fair exchange for the jet lag, bad food, airport shuffles, and general uneasiness that goes along with cruising the friendly skies. Getting on the plane was the first step in a tedious three-legged journey back to Montana. And there is no easy way to get there from the Buffalo International Airport. If I were going to England, that would be different. I suppose it's not really so bad: Buffalo to Detroit to Minneapolis to Bozeman, and then an hour-and-a-half drive to Twin Bridges. Because of gaining two time zones, I'd be home well before dark. In the northern Rockies, the days start getting quite long in early May.

The three weeks went rather quickly on this particular eastern tour with a dual purpose. The grand celebration of my folks' fiftieth wedding anniversary should have been enough justification for the trip, but the event was sandwiched between fishing junkets to Ontario and Michigan designed to provide more information for the book my brother and I had been writing about Great Lakes steelhead for quite some time. This joint venture had been a common goal of ours for a decade. Although researching nomadic steelhead may sound like a good deal on the surface, after years of covering every square inch of the massive Great Lakes basin, the glamour of the project had worn a bit thin. In for a penny, in for a pound, as they say, for if there were any misgivings about the effort, it was too late to turn back. I swore as I was boarding the plane, the steelhead I had landed on the lower Niagara only a few hours beforehand was the last fish I wanted to see for a while.

I took my usual window seat and waited. If all went according to schedule, a generic elderly woman who looked a lot like everybody's grandmother would take her seat next to me at any moment now. It happened every time. I have spent many flights looking at pictures and listening to detailed biographies of children and children's children. Sure enough, a few minutes later *there she was*—about ten rows forward and checking out seat numbers. No need for that, I thought. All she had to do was to find me. This time I was wrong, though, but only about one thing. The lady didn't look like everybody's grandmother—just like everybody's aunt. Middle-aged and attired in an understated trench coat, she was lugging along that type of paper shopping bag with two small string handles. It was stuffed with trinkets, some half-sewn items, and a book or two. She took the seat right next to mine and looked at me timidly. Barely smiling, she then pulled out one of those romance novels and proceeded to read it straight through to Detroit. Not even a peep.

Taking advantage of the opportunity, I caught up on a few notes, watched as the north shore of Lake Erie guided our flight, and reflected on the fifty-year marriage of my parents. They were sure surprised upon entering a room full of faces from the past along with tears of joy amid the standard "where has all the time gone?" comments. For my brother, sister, and myself, giving back in the form of a party somehow seemed inadequate for the lifetime of giving they shared with us. But judging from their faces, my folks were humbly overwhelmed with happiness. Maybe good people do get rewarded in the end, as it is said, with riches far beyond wealth. For my parents, that would be more than enough.

I couldn't help thinking that they probably were a bit puzzled with the life direction of their eldest son. An itinerant fisherman wasn't exactly what they had in mind years ago when they were paying for my education. And though Mom would have wished that I continued to teach for a career, she never expressed much disappointment, as long as I was happy. Additionally, Dad always seemed proud that I was able to find so many ways to travel from one beautiful part of the continent to another in search of something to catch on a fly. He doesn't understand fly fishing, but he does understand travel. The longing is always reflected in his recounts of World War II, his assignment to the Fiji Islands, and his jaunt through India. Dad's desire to explore the world was interrupted by raising a family after the war, never again to be totally realized. Trips to visit me in Utah, Idaho and Montana were as close as he'd ever get. Somehow, it seems, my travels have vicariously fulfilled the dreams he had for himself a long time ago.

My eyes were barely starting to close when we came in for a landing in Detroit. A jump from one end of Lake Erie to the other ends in forty-five minutes. I said good-bye to my travel mate—and thanked her. The layover in Detroit Metro is brief, hardly providing enough time to walk across the dingy, crowded thoroughfare to make the connecting shuttle to Minneapolis. The urge to grab a fast-food burger on the way was compounded by the knowledge that there were no meals on either of the remaining flights back to Bozeman. I would barely have enough time, and I'd have to act quickly. As I got in line, an attractive young counter girl mumbled something in my direction. "Excuse me?" was my somewhat distracted reply. A rather terse, "I axed jou, whad jou want?" was the Ebonic retort that came from her unhappy-looking face. In fact, the whole crew appeared annoyed that work was interrupting their plans for the day. Such oppression could be justified, I suppose, if their collective age didn't average less than eighteen years. I just took whatever burger was available and found a quiet corner to gulp it down. The soggy, warm slab of meat had apparently been sitting around for a while, and the fact that it was covered with about a half-inch of oozing mayo dripping from its edges made it that much less appealing. My mouth worked quicker than my brain, though, and within a few minutes I was headed for the boarding gate stuffed with the reason that fast-food joints will continue to exist until the end of time.

This plane was big, seats everywhere, and people were packed into the carrier like a herd of Montana beef crammed into a cattle truck headed for market. The Minneapolis-St. Paul Airport is a Northwest Airline hub to the west, so this shuttle of humanity continued with regularity throughout the day. When I located my customary window position, I was surprised to see *a man* already occupying the neighboring seat. Next to him sat a well-dressed lady with big hair and generous layers of make-up, presumably his wife. Excusing myself, I crawled my way past the woman and over the guy, plopping down next to a window that gave full view of the wing and little else. "Howdy" was the word that came from the seat next to mine, a friendly spark with a touch of southern drawl. "The name is William Raymond Elsworth, but my friends all call me Billy Ray."

Billy Ray was decked out in a conservative blue suit and black tie, and he displayed a small fortune of gold dangling from his extremities. His precisely combed hair looked more like an acrylic helmet. Once blond, but now blended with gray, every strand was epoxied neatly into place. Along with well-manicured fingernails, he was doused with enough cologne to blow up the entire plane if he ever got near a match.

"*My* friends call me Jerry," I chimed in while reflexively giving him a business card conveniently extracted from the pocket of my flannel shirt. His wife could not have been less interested in the proceedings. With the information he extracted from my handout, he turned toward me. "So you make fishing poles," he twanged with a smile that was as plastic as his hair. "Fly rods," I interjected, but he continued as if he didn't hear me. He talked of catching bass out of some Tennessee farm pond in his younger day, years before God called him to serve as a Baptist minister. Through the ramblings of where he had been, why he was there, and where he is going, I also learned that he taught theology at some college in the South. Uh-oh. I could see where this conversation was going. When I told him that I once dabbled in a similar calling for a while—Catholic style—his pontification barely skipped a beat. The words just rolled out like a Sunday morning sermon.

Sure enough, our discussion turned to "the Lord" as the air bus began to taxi into position on the runway behind eighteen other planes. He preached about the need for us all to be reborn in the Lord. Interrupting, I told him politely that I meant no disrespect to him or several of my still-clergy friends, but the subject of the Lord made me very uncomfortable in this era of big-business religion. Adding, without getting into the intimate details of my experiences, that the hypocrisy, self righteousness, and greed associated with organized religion turned me off years ago.

My problem is with the modern-day messengers—but, certainly, not the Christian message. Somewhere in time, the big picture has been lost. Over the span of two thousand years, the point surely has been missed.

Choosing my words carefully, I deliberated, "Nowadays this whole religious affair seems like a carnival, everyone pitching the best Lord for the buck. From my perspective, I'm not really sure the Lord would see much worth saving anymore."

His look turned solemn, "God our Savior desires all men to be saved. Timothy, chapter two, verses three through four. "

Maybe so, I told him, but I didn't believe—at least for me— memorizing Scripture passages or kneeling in a house of dogma on Sunday mornings was the answer. With that, Billy Ray began to move uncomfortably in his seat. He didn't see me as a threat, or even as a challenge, but just as someone he really wasn't interested in talking to anymore.

It was my turn to pontificate, so when I mentioned that some of the most well-adjusted, good people I have ever met were folks who weren't overwhelmed by the emotions associated with organized religion somewhere in their lives, Billy Ray just closed his eyes. I did concede, though, that there were also many good people who regularly participate in many forms of worship, my folks included, but that approach to life may not be for everyone. My wife, I told him, does more good works for people than anyone I had ever met, and she has never gone to church. In many ways, she was a saint.

Billy Ray then proclaimed, "But unless she acknowledges the Lord, all those good works will go for naught. She will not be saved." Although I never really understood the concept behind "being saved," he quoted something else from the Bible to justify his position. His all-knowing demeanor was impressive in a pompous sort of way.

"I suppose you are going to tell me," I hypothetically challenged, "that if a guy like Charles Manson does acknowledge the Lord sometime in his prison existence, he will be saved, even if he is not doing anything profound for his fellow human beings."

"It's not for us to judge," replied the Reverend Billy. "The Lord works in strange ways."

"Too strange for me," I told him. "Doing the right things for the right reasons is the secret to a happy existence — and possibly, eternal bliss." I then added, "I'm quite sure Christ would agree." After concluding that I'd rather take my chances on being a good person, going fishing on Sundays, and being faithful to my pagan wife, Billy Ray turned to "Tammy Faye." As far as he was concerned, I was a lost cause.

Somewhere over Lake Michigan it hit me, but I don't believe the discomfort had anything to do with God's retribution. With a pain in the gut like a kick from a mule, and a cranial cavity that was in danger of exploding, the revenge of the killer mayonnaise had apparently descended upon me. Ptomaine, salmonella, who knew? At this point I'll refrain from the concept of e. coli since you can't say anything directly about hamburgers anymore. You know how those Texans are about beef these days. Say anything you want, for instance, about the president; but chose your words very carefully when it comes to a chunk of meat. Just ask Oprah. I didn't want Billy Ray to see me squirm, though—couldn't give him that satisfaction—but I needed off that plane, and quickly.

Woozy, weak, and wandering the Minneapolis airport, I found the restrooms. The plane for Bozeman was boarding when I arrived at its gate of departure. Given the present status of my health, the thought of two more hours entrapped in an elbow-room-only container inspired near panic. I caught a break, though; there was no man of the cloth, no elderly lady. There was nobody in the row of assigned seats next to mine, and they stayed empty as the plane headed westward on the last leg of the journey. Fargo was just coming into the panorama beyond the right wing when the siege began; a wave of vengeance hit. Fortunately, the toilets were a direct shot from where I was sitting. Returning to my seat, I closed my eyes and started to count the minutes.

I dozed, teetering on the brink of total annihilation, but suspended, ironically, in a merciful dreamlike embrace—until thoughts flooded back about the trip. It seems I could only remember the bad points. Pleasant thoughts are difficult to conjure in times of desperation. Twenty-two steelhead hooked in Michigan's Big Manistee, three landed. How could something like that happen? Not that landing fish is really important, but the string of bad luck annoyed me then, and it was haunting me now. The words eloquently stated by the Alonzo Hagen character in Richard Brautigan's classic *Trout Fishing in America* usually come to me during streaks of poor fishing, but they seemed particularly appropriate on this occasion. "...I've lost every trout I've ever hooked." After losing fish in every way possible for seven years, Alonzo concluded that "it was an interesting experiment in total loss." He finally resolved that someone else would have to go trout fishing, but it wasn't going to be him. At this point in my physical quandary, I could totally relate to his words. Fishing ever again seemed but a remote possibility. Amen, Alonzo.

The last hour of the ordeal dragged on and on, without much relief. Finding some comfort in looking ahead to my arrival in Montana, I figured the plane would land in Bozeman at about four-thirty. Once there, I would greet my wife, visit the restroom, gather my gear, visit the restroom again, and, with a bit of luck, be sacked out in the peaceful sanctuary of my bedroom by six thirty. There I could ride out the balance of this food poisoning mambo. And though we landed on schedule, the rest of the plan went awry. My wife was nowhere in sight.

Sitting next to the restroom with a pile of luggage and equipment, I waited. In my condition, time took on an exaggerated dimension of slow motion. Seconds were minutes, and minutes clicked on for what seemed like hours. Debra was not usually late. But maybe this was her way of getting back at me for my consistent tardiness over the years. If I have one flaw, it would be the automatic one or two extra hours my local fishing outings would extend beyond my promised time of return. It never failed, and over two decades, we had developed an understanding. But if it was her intention to make a point, Debra couldn't have picked a worse situation to do so. It was then I promised myself to reform, to mend my ways, to become more responsible—anything! The lesson had been learned. After an hour, though, I began to worry.

Just then Debra walked into the airport, looking a bit hassled. She couldn't help but notice my decrepit condition, and I filled her in on the grizzly details. She then apologized for her late arrival, and though it didn't have anything to do with scaring me straight, I could tell she had already cooked up a pretty good excuse. It seems she had decided to shun the interstate on the way from Twin Bridges in favor of the scenic roundabout route through Ennis to Norris, along the lower Madison River for a while, and then to Belgrade where the Bozeman airport is actually located. Here it comes, I thought. In a tone of frenzy right out of one of those low-budget horror films, she gasped, "All those bugs!" When she had reached the section of highway that paralleled the river, "*All those bugs* were everywhere! They were crawling on the highway and whacking the windshield. Clouds and clouds of bugs." When she had tried to use the windshield wiper, the greasy critters smudged the glass with an impenetrable film that was impossible to see through. The way she told it, it took two pit stops to clean a peep hole using river water, a rag, and windshield fluid so she could continue driving safely through the barrage. I had to hand it to her; as far as excuses went, this one topped the list. And it certainly piqued my curiosity, even in my downtrodden state of existence.

When we arrived in the parking lot, I could smell Debra's car before I saw it. Just as I suspected, and it was just two days after Mother's Day. When the car came into full view, it was a sight. Smudged, squashed and splattered, *Brachycentrus occidentalis*—in other words, the Mother's Day caddis—were caked everywhere. Their little bodies plastered the entire car. Their contorted, mottled wings were either sticking up or hanging down, and thousands of green egg sacks were blotched in a display of free form modern art with an overtone of contemporary surrealism. The aromatic sweetness emitted by these breeding insects emanated the fragrance of a cheap perfume, likely sickening even to a nose attached to a healthy body. It was six p.m. "Let's take the scenic route home," I suggested as my mind began to distance itself from the discomfort of my body.

"How about some Pepto Bismol?" she asked.

"Heck with that," I answered. "It will be dark soon!"

A half an hour later, the lower Madison River showed itself in the distance. This piece of water has become the playground for the throngs responsible for Bozeman's population explosion over recent years. It is distinguished from the upper Madison by the archaic power dam at the head of the Bear Trap Canyon Wilderness Area. The water behind the dam creates Ennis Lake, a shallow impoundment that heats up considerably during the summer and, at times, provides water to the lower Madison that is too warm for salmonids. Although this section still supports decent populations of trout, it is not without a struggle. As we got closer to the river, caddis were crawling everywhere. We stopped the car along the river at a convenient pull over.

This caddis event often associated with Mother's Day is an odd affair. Although it is probably most famous on the Yellowstone River near Livingston, many other rivers receive this early season hatch in various degrees as well. Unfortunately, when it gets warm enough to induce a massive emergence of the grannom, it is also warm enough to start melting the snow in the mountains. So, depending on the amount of the white stuff in the hills and the altitude at which it still exists, these factors determine just how long the hatch will be fishable. Often, in a day or two, the river gets high and dirty. Also, the water temperature drops at the same time because of the inflowing ice water. As a result, these changing conditions put a serious damper on the angler's chances to significantly "cash in" on the event. Consequently, when you hear about the hatch, it is usually too late. Over the years, I could have won the You-Should-Have-Been-Here-Yesterday Award many times over when it comes to this highly touted Mother's Day phenomenon.

So when I looked at the clear water pulsing through the Madison, the swarms of caddis bouncing up and down everywhere, and all the willing fish recklessly slurping in the apparent feast, I fully understood the uniqueness of the situation.

As I reflected upon the words of Alonzo Hagen, I also recalled the promise made to myself earlier in the day about not wanting to see another fish for a while. But then I dismissed these thoughts as irrational musings. I turned to Debra and, after careful consideration of my health predicament, sheepishly pleaded, "Just one cast?"

"I thought you were sick," she said in a tone that implied wifely concern.

"Maybe it's the fresh air, maybe it's the caddis, but I think I'm cured. It's a miracle!" Although I know my wife is a saint, I didn't think she had those kinds of powers. At that point, I truly wondered what had happened to the malady that afflicted me for most of the afternoon.

"Go ahead," she conceded with no strings attached. "But you can make more than one cast. I brought a book." She knows me only too well.

And as I approached the river, I hoped that somewhere on his pilgrimage to save lost souls, Billy Ray was praying for ours... you know, just in case.

The Years of the Cat

Cats are a lot like bowling or broccoli—either folks like them or they don't. I never really formed an opinion about cats—just never really thought about them much, I guess—until a friend's tabby had a litter of five kittens in 1977. The runt was slate gray and so small she barely covered half of my palm when I placed this cute, newborn creature in my hand. She was a gritty survivor, too. Right from the start, she had to struggle and jostle for a feeding position, and muscling out siblings that were twice her size wasn't an easy task. At that point in my life, I never had any great desire to have a pet for an on-the-road-sidekick, but if I followed the example of many other friends, the choice would surely have been that of the canine persuasion. Nevertheless, the decision to embark upon the path of cat ownership for the first time ever came quite naturally after admiring this diminutive feline's spirit and tenacity.

Although it took years to comprehend the ramifications of this commitment, my newly acquired dependent learned quickly to adapt to an offbeat lifestyle. Stormy, as I named her, enjoyed traveling, especially when the road led to a river or lake. In the process, she became an unlikely, but extraordinary, fishing companion. Not only did her undercoat provide a constant supply of gray dubbing for a number of fly patterns, but she always seemed very interested in fish. I didn't realize how interested, though, until I found the remnant tails of two kokanee salmon I had stashed in the cooler one day for *my* dinner later that evening. Although she did escape my wrath after a stern explanation of the rules, she continued to live on life's edge from that day forward. As she pushed the concept of "nine lives" beyond the limits of reason, the survival skills she learned very early in life served her well throughout a prosperous existence.

Traveling with a cat had some serious drawbacks, and these became evident immediately. The restrictions of a small pickup most certainly cramped Stormy's lifestyle, and whenever the slightest opportunity to break for wide-open spaces became available, off she would bolt into the unknown. This wasn't usually a problem in an out-of-the-way campground, but then late one June there was the moonlit night on Highway 10 near Philipsburg, Montana. After a day fishing Flint Creek, "the cat," fueled by the energy only a full moon could provide, decided to boldly play center line chicken with the Saturday night bar crowd traffic. With graceful quickness, she deftly moved like a gray streak, tempting fate and winning all the hair-raising challenges with Chevy and Ford pickups until a sudden surge of boredom brought her into the range of capture. Though most of her binges weren't as dramatic, it was only a few years later when this Evel Knievel of the cat world accepted her next great challenge—a Burlington Northern freight train on a late-night gallop down the tracks near Montana's Kootenai River. With more than gentle persuasion and great consternation, Stormy came to her senses without incident before the scenario played itself out. In an evening filled with high intrigue and suspense, the diesel's whistle blew to signal its impending arrival just as the cat settled in for a restful nap.

Cats can fit through holes the size of a golf ball, particularly when freedom is at stake. This cat fact was discovered after a late-evening grocery junket at an all-night store in Missoula. Every summer weekend during those days was spent fishing throughout western Montana. These jaunts would usually end Sunday at midnight with a regular stop for weekly provisions. Then it was off to Idaho's Powell Ranger Station, and work, for the next five days. Once the chore had been completed, it was customary to check the cat's food and water before heading over Lolo Pass; but that night, all this check revealed was no cat and the smallest of openings torn in the camper's window screen. After an hour's search on the busy streets of the city, it seemed all hope was gone. Serious deliberation dictated a distasteful decision. Getting a refund for the just-purchased king-size bag of cat food and hitting the road seemed like the only option at that hour. With some luck, maybe she would turn up at the pet shelter during the week.

When I sadly approached the checkout counter, the young lady at the register was still buzzing about the gray cat that had been running through the aisles of the store for the past hour, an indication of the giddy level of amusement in the world of groceries at that time of night. Recounting my unhappy tale, I then inquired how this "mystery cat" quandry had been resolved. It seemed that after the night manager and a merry band of stock clerks finally corralled the frisky fur ball, one of the helpers was ordered to transport her to an alley about a mile from the store. In what can only be termed a supreme expression of "customer service," I was lead by an apologetic but spacey crew of three summer stock boys to an alley behind a closed bar, and the search began. For Stormy, the hide-and-go-seek continued well into the morning as we occasionally caught a glimpse of her yellow eyes reflecting the glint of the back alley lights. The game ended only when the cat got tired of playing. She had great fun! The cat and I finally headed back to Idaho hours later than planned.

Being a responsible pet owner is an important ingredient in maintaining the natural settings that surround us. Training Stormy not to chase birds was a tediously successful challenge, though, conversely, the birds enjoyed a free rein chasing her. Reluctantly settling into the role of house cat when not on the road, she could even make the occasional stroll around the yard an adventure. In the fields surrounding the cabin in the backwoods of northern Idaho where we wintered, she developed a healthy respect for nature early in life. Upon responding to her distress call one autumn morning, there she was, timidly cowering under the pickup while a beautiful northern goshawk perched upon the truck's boat rack, obviously just missing out on lunch. Stormy was unharmed, but she always kept one eye on the sky from that day on, while possibly keeping a close tally. "Hmm, now what life was that, three or four?"

Northern Idaho was unforgiving as hawks, owls, coyotes, and the occasional bear ruled. After surviving a brief encounter with a great horned owl, Stormy resolved that being a house cat was not a bad option at all. While recovering from her wounds, it probably occurred to her that keeping an eye to the night sky was sound wisdom also. She learned that her survival depended upon conforming to the ways of nature.

The years went by, and the cat matured. Eventually marriage entered the picture, and so did a rotund Lhasa apso. It was a package deal! Since fishing vagaries took us in many directions, my wife and I, along with the cat and dog, traveled coast to coast several times. From Maine to New York, to California and even into Canada, as well, friends, relatives and fishermen got to know this friendly cat, but one by one Stormy's nine lives continued to dwindle. She survived a several-day disappearance in the Bay Area and a tangle with a closing garage door in New York. Upon pulling out of a campground in South Dakota, a brief final glance in the rearview mirror revealed that, indeed, the gray object standing on the picnic table that cold November morning was "the cat."

Stormy was still up to her tricks even into her fifteenth year, this time on a fall fishing trip to the Great Lakes. She once again sneaked out of a camper door after an overnight stop in Wyoming, and her departure wasn't discovered until a breakfast stop in Casper over a hundred miles later. In a desperate panic, we returned to miles of endless nowhere defined by sprawling sagebrush-covered hills and lined by the world's longest continuous fence. Since we stopped in the dark the night before at an undefined pullover and started again in the dark that morning, the sameness of the landscape was particularly unfamiliar as the search for the cat took on futility of monumental proportions. Out of hundreds of empty square miles, one clump of roadside weeds looked vaguely familiar, and it was there we began the search. It must have been the year of the cat, for it wasn't long before the familiar meow echoed across the hills as a bewildered, perplexed gray cat attached to the sound strolled into full view and, with great humility, headed straight for the truck. For several hours, Stormy, no doubt, had an opportunity to again ponder life's meaning—this time, Wyoming style.

Anyone who has had an enduring relationship with any animal knows the value of a pet's unconditional friendship and wordless understanding. Throughout the years, I learned much about nature, myself, and even life itself through the eyes of my cat. There is a balance between mankind and nature that must be achieved to ensure harmony on earth; for on a planet full of people, life has to be a cooperative effort between responsible humans and all other beings. Stormy had lived a good life, a fulfilled cat life, while defying many odds and dodging numerous bullets along the way.

The life of a good pet often passes much too quickly, and it is never easy when the inevitable comes. In the middle of her seventeenth year, Stormy finally gave up her ninth life. On just an average day in early March, a troublesome dog pried open a gate, invaded the sanctuary of our fenced Montana yard, and savagely attacked the world's friendliest cat. When I finally got to the point of the conflict, there lay my longtime fishing companion and friend. She was barely breathing. We had been through a lot together, fished many streams, and I thanked her. A victim not of nature or even natural causes, her life then ended the same way it began seventeen years before—but this time, cradled in my arms. I always envisioned this cat of greatness dying a noble death, but in the end she succumbed to a neglected neighborhood mutt in a matter of minutes. Her passing seemed so ordinary, yet the sadness was so profound. After spending over one-third of my years with this amiable being, it was only at death that I realized how significantly an animal can touch one's life. Loyal companionship, whether it be animal or human, is a treasure not easily replaced.

Years come and go. All things change. To have had an opportunity for such a relationship was truly fortunate. It is said that life goes on; but the void created by her absence continues on, as well. Adjusting to the loss was very difficult, and sometimes, late at night, I still see her hiding in the shadows of a darkened room.

But for Fortune

A perfect fish in a perfect world, the beautiful cutthroat trout swims in the crystalline reverberations springing from the earth's inner soul. To all who regularly wallow in the silted cauldron of life's lowland rivers, these ribbons flow forth from a higher source, beckoning the enlightened to partake in their cleansing waters of renewal. It is there, in these forgotten reaches, that many specialized forms of the cutthroat species adorn the lost recesses of the West. Like wildflowers with fins, these trout are rugged, but delicate enough to wilt in the presence of man's infidelity to the land and to the water that breathe a spirituality sought in the silent dimensions of heart, mind, and body. While the many variations of this fish—Lahontan, Snake River, Yellowstone, Rio Grande, westslope, coastal, etc.—substantiate the species' resilient ability to adapt and meld to the geological whims that span the millennia, the very existence of these wondrously sensitive creatures still offers a small degree of hope that something is right wherever modest populations continue to exist.

By quirk of its innocence, however, the cutthroat has been victimized throughout its range. Where this occurs, the species simply chooses not to exist in the aftermath of human abuse.

Belittled also by those who should most appreciate these jewels, many who fish the untainted reaches of its realm mistake the cutthroat's naiveté as a tragic flaw and, in human terms, such traits are unacceptable. But in a perfect world, things are what they seem. Even a perfect fish needs to eat, and when they do, they do so perfectly. A sterile but balanced high country environment provides a stingy food source, and only the most capable of inhabitants have adapted to these rigors. Every offering from pine needles to mayflies caught up in the current of shimmering clarity is closely inspected, carefully examined before it is judged sufficient, and then efficiently taken with delicate precision. Succumbing repeatedly to a well-tied buggy-looking fly is not necessarily a character weakness, either. This is a species of wishful survival instincts, but only if the environs within which it dwells remain conducive to living the life it knows. Most importantly, these beings are a vital component of the vanishing vastness that threatens the extinction of our very souls, or at the very least, act as indicators of this diminished quality. All too often the waters of purity reflecting these lost truths float by us unnoticed, like a gentle tear, until it is too late.

The indicators were unmistakable in the waters of northern Idaho near and around the town of Priest River. A long journey in search of something that made sense led me to this dead-end town in the mid-seventies. I had hoped that hanging out in the winter hills, secluded in a small cabin, would provide a revelation that would point me in the right direction. I needed to be touched by something untouched. But to my disappointment, this land of beautiful waters had been desecrated decades beforehand. Years of habitat degradation and backwoods thinking destroyed massive populations of cutthroat and Dolly Varden (now bull trout) without a twinge of conscience. Kept alive in the minds of the local old-timers responsible, in part, for the demise of a unique strain of westslope cutthroat, lower Priest River and the adjoining Pend Oreille River were nothing more than mausoleums containing only the memory of a fish that could not adapt to the desecration.

Upon moving to the Lochsa River region of Idaho in 1976, the disappointment continued, though it seemed unimaginable that man's impact could be so evident in such close proximity to the gateway of the Selway-Bitterroot Wilderness Area. The United States forest that borders the wilderness paid the price for this privilege. Inordinate timber quotas, the usual political trade-off, was the price paid for barring the logging contingent, with saws ablazing, from plundering an important quantity of land that fell within the wilderness. Blatant was the pride responsible for the prowess of destruction that led to yet another corner of perfection falling prey to the hands of humans. Adjacent to the wilderness, many mountainsides exhibited disfiguring scars, the battle wounds attributed to decades of the worst sort of logging practices. Likewise, the river paralleled by Highway 12 was easily stripped of its finned treasures by the same inane ignorance. So far removed from human scrutiny, the out-of-sight-out-of-mind philosophy that led to the great degradation of many headwaters throughout the West was displayed prominently in the Lochsa's upper reaches.

The Lochsa River is paralleled its entire length by the only major highway that cuts east-west through central Idaho. On the side to the south, the same river is bounded by wilderness, and it is viewed like a panoramic mural from the highway for over forty miles. Perfect on one side, imperfect on the other; a flowing oxymoron, this sad contradiction well symbolizes man's relentless battle with nature. Although there were certainly negative impacts from logging abuse in a portion of its headwater regions, the influence from its wilderness heritage tended to mitigate the Lochsa's potential damage. The river's name, given by the native Nez Perce, means "rough waters," and this descriptive depiction was sure to refer to the chutes of white water ripping within its confines as the mountains shed their snowy mantles in the warm breath of the late spring rains. During summer months, the Lochsa is not quite so forbidding as it steps its way, pool by pool, up to the confluence of the two tributaries—Crooked Fork Creek and White Sand Creek—that mark its origin. Orange and reddish-tan rocks of varying size combine with golden gravel to give the river a slightly stained appearance. Yet when the water collects in pools, its transformation to an emerald hue in the gathering depths provides a mysterious security to the westslope cutthroat that continue to dwell there to this day. During the late seventies, it took innovative management techniques to restore the numbers of fish depleted from the endless onslaught of roadside anglers, and these regulations are still in place. From the cutthroat's point of view, apparently, there is still much right about the Lochsa; the perfect fish, however, has had to learn to adapt to a certain level of imperfections. In some cases, an uneasy compromise is the only solution.

The more I got to know the area, the more my disillusionment gradually dwindled, and I learned to adapt to the imperfections as well. Despite it all, there were few places in the lower forty eight states that compared. The Powell Ranger Station was the only community for many miles in either direction. Most folks who lived in this sparsely populated region either worked in governmental positions for the U.S. Forest Service and the State of Idaho, or at the private Lochsa Lodge. Living in a fish bowl and working in relative solitude year-round can be unnerving for many, but in the shadow of the wilderness there arose an undeniable allure, a magical sense of attachment to something special. It seemed everyone associated with the area was there because of this kinship with nature. For me, ending up at the outer limits of civilization was yet another in a series of chance events that seemed destined to have a meaningful consequence. I was still running from the confusion of the late sixties, and a bout with a life-threatening ulcer during that time was indication enough that a conventional lifestyle was not for me. I came to "find myself." And no matter how trite that cliché has become over the years, the truth remains that, until one can achieve some sort of inner harmony with one's self, and balance *that* with the rest of life, it is difficult to attain the contentment that leads to sanity. This is intensely individual stuff, but eventually everyone has to dance to the music they make. In a way, I came to the Lochsa to write my song.

Unlike the northern parts of Idaho, the mid to late seventies was a good period to experience this part of the world. It was apparent that many others were looking for something at that time also, and the questions that spurred the intellectual revolution of the late sixties started to influence forgotten corners of earth's realities by the end of the decade. The power and greed that led to the wanton and wasteful destruction of our renewable natural resources were finally examined and brought to judgment. The ugly side of the American Way, exposed during the Viet Nam fiasco, was also seriously challenged during this period, but cutting off the many heads of the monster would take years. The demand for a cleaner environment and accountability for those destroying it led to much-improved logging practices. And the Clean Water Act enacted during that same period is directly responsible for the quality fisheries we have today. In a bold move for those days, one of the first catch-and-release areas *ever* was instituted on the Lochsa River in 1977. Though many locals protested by not fishing the forty miles within the regulated section for years, a few of us had the rare experience to witness the rebirth of a wonderful population of westslopes with fly rod in hand and no one in sight.

The government job that occupied my days was nothing to write home about, but it kept me on the outskirts of humanity. As a compliance inspector, my principal assignment was to make sure logging roads were built and maintained to the strictest of new environmental standards. As long as these roads continued to be built, someone had to make sure they were constructed in the least threatening manner. The logging contingent was intimidating, but the foremen of several outfits I worked with already had forestry degrees, thus reflecting the changing times. Protecting watersheds and drainages became a primary focus and, despite the occasional locking of horns, everyone involved believed in the needs that prompted new forestry policies. In particular, one foreman for a major lumber company, a born and raised Montana fly fisherman, welcomed this approach; it relieved him from wrestling with his conscience. In fact, as our respect for each other grew, he divulged several of his secret spots (in a day when there were secret spots) on a few of his favorite Montana rivers. Based upon this information, countless weekends were spent over the years expanding fishing horizons to include the legendary waters located within a reachable weekend distance on the Montana side of Lolo Pass.

The freedom to experience an unencumbered existence was exhilarating, but the real opportunity for enlightenment took on many varied forms within the vicinity of Idaho's wilderness. Weekday afternoons spent exploring the Lochsa and its tributaries for Dolly Varden, small juvenile steelhead, and cutthroat unveiled many truths. The greenish, silvery sleek westslope, sparsely spotted at the tail and sporting a red tinge on its gill plate and belly, was captivating, and my appreciation for this fish never wavered. Close comparison to the many other forms of the species throughout the West revealed many characteristic differences, as well as variations in color, shape, and behavior. To my untrained eye, there also seemed to be subtle differences in the westslope form of the species found throughout Montana, Idaho, and British Columbia; but such hairsplitting seemed senseless. The fascinating study of this small niche in nature revealed a deeper truth: insight is the result of understanding, and much can be understood by taking the time to stop, look, and listen to "the within" of everything. By paying attention to the smallest of inner details, the clearer the big picture becomes; therein lies the conundrum of life.

As for the people of the Lochsa, there was a camaraderie shared by most of the area's regulars based on familiarity, and a common belief in wild spaces. Like a cast of characters in an ongoing play, everyone had a part to play. I saw my role as that of an observer, on the outside looking in. But that's the way I wanted it. The lifeblood and driving force for most inhabitants was the yearlong anticipation for the beginning of elk season. For many, it ended the same day it began. It seemed everyone knew exactly where to be on opening day and, once a bull was shot, the yearning curiously began to build again for next season. I favored fishing because, to tell the truth, a year is a long time to yearn. There were some wonderful folks I'll always remember, and some I've been quick to forget. It's rare to be treated fairly at a job, but my superiors were honorable people, and so were the few individuals I could call my friends.

Rising above the melange of characters was a bit player who, in the end, impacted many of our lives. My relationship with Jim fell into the ships-passing-in-the-night category. When we met, Jim was a part of a hippie commune, the Brush Flowers, that had bid for and won a brush piling contract from the government. In July, 1978, an assignment taking me on a twenty-mile trek into a developing timber sale was temporarily waylaid by the sight of this ragtag group. Sitting along the roadside, next to their multicolored flower bus, they were passing around a reefer. Upon stopping my government vehicle to say hello, they kindly offered me a hit. Though I believed deeply in what these people symbolized, and in appearance could have qualified for initiation into their group, one of my best virtues is discretion. I kindly replied "no" and asked if they needed some assistance. They briefly explained the job they were doing, or were supposed to be doing. Informing me that the group got paid *only* for work they completed correctly, the commune had collectively adopted a pace suitable for the "laid back" lifestyle. I might add, they weren't about to apologize for it either. Spending some government time building rapport with these castoffs from the late sixties seemed a wise idea, so we chatted for a while. To a certain degree, I could relate to their cause because of spending a good portion of the sixties and early seventies in a commune of sorts, working for a better world through a religious misadventure. But when my idealism finally gave way to disillusionment, I began to wander, and fishing became the only anchor that kept me from drifting off into nihilism. Feeling as lost as these folks looked, we exchanged thoughts and ideas. Maybe they had found the answer, the key to the Secret Garden. It was worth the few moments to find out.

Before continuing onward, I had met everyone in the group. Calculating who was paired with whom, there were a few I couldn't quite figure out. Neil and Joan were among the latter. Neil was a trim, energetic longhair with extensive degrees from several western universities. Joan was an attractive, nubile-looking young gal with the maturity of the teenager she still appeared to be. Neil was hot on her trail, though there was nothing official about their relationship. Lastly there was Jim, a wilder-looking character than all the others. And though his eyes revealed substantial depth, his demeanor was aloof. Obviously high on homegrown and God only knows what else, there was something unsettling about the glimpses of true character squeezing through what had not yet been totally wasted. He wanted to talk alone. And so we did for a while. He was too far gone to establish meaningful contact, but to me he was like a mirror. A left turn instead of a right somewhere in the past, and I could have been Jim.

Throughout the season, our paths occasionally crossed in the oddest places. In fact, Jim was the only Brush Flower I would ever see. Whenever we met, he seemed eager to talk, while directing the conversation as if to size me up. Government worker, friend or foe? Often, any discussion would invariably turn to The

War, and Jim's anger and hate toward the government frequently surfaced in a mercurial flash. We both agreed that there was no greater manifestation of man's stupidity than war. The realization that this war had everything to do with big business profits and absolutely nothing else didn't help Jim's disposition either. Our fathers had fought a war, saved the world, and become heroes. They grew into men in the process. In a perverse sort of way, they wanted us to have that same opportunity. But the baby boomer crowd, prepped for college since birth, never could buy into the inane propaganda. As far as Jim was concerned, the "fear of communism" amounted to a sinister bogeyman contrived to perpetuate the need for an immorally conceived defense budget. Hence, the intellectualization behind the voices of the sixties that changed forever the way our country operates paled the conventional right wing "wisdom" of the day. Sent involuntarily to Viet Nam, Jim once confided that he couldn't close his eyes at night anymore.

During the sixties, virtually everyone had to make decisions in life reacting to an absurd and awful event that hung over our heads like a shroud, violating the consciousness of our youthful minds. Children were expected to make choices that could affect their futures forever at a time when they should have been full of life, and full of dreams. Under such duress, no one was capable of making a decision in the best interest of anything, yet somehow we all did; and somehow we have to live with those decisions. Spending eight years in the seminary was my way of coping, but in the final analysis, it was eight years lost. The innocence of our youth was blatantly stolen from us for the most selfish of reasons, and I often wonder if it is the stifled dreams of my younger years that I, too, have been looking for.

Crooked Fork Creek is the northern fork of the Lochsa, and some nice cutthroat and Dolly Varden always seemed to show up there in September. The dry fly usually gives way to streamers late in the season, as the midafternoon disappearance of the sun behind the tight mountainscape brings a crisp coolness to the evening air. After another fine outing in my element, the hike up from the stream and the subsequent drive out on the backroad put me onto the highway in total darkness. Avoiding moose on the move was always an important driving tactic, especially at that time of year when the mating urge instinctively locked these 1,500-pound beasts into autopilot. So I proceeded cautiously, eyes glued to the vista. About a mile down the highway, my peripheral vision detected distinct movement in the rightside ditch. I slowed down just enough to evaluate the situation. But it wasn't a moose, or any other animal for that matter. It was Jim, or an apparition that looked like Jim, climbing onto the road with what turned out to be a Winchester lever action rifle in his hands.

Curious, I slowly pulled over, and then safely stopped about one hundred yards past where I had seen him. I yelled out the rolled-down window into the darkness, "What's going on, Jim?" There was no answer. But just then, without a sound, he materialized next to the truck sporting a strange smile. Too dumbfounded to be scared, I added, "And what the hell are you doing on the highway after dark with that rifle?" Somewhat disjointed, he told me that he had been hunting. Though hunting season had not yet begun, I wasn't about to argue. We were ten miles from the lodge. "Get in," I urged, "and we'll go for coffee."

The ride there was silent, but Jim was visibly distraught and obviously spaced into the ozone somewhere. I should have been more careful, but I also believe in lending a helping hand when I can. As we ordered up the coffee, he muttered something like, "They taught me how to kill." After my emphatic "*What?*" he somberly continued to divulge how his Special Forces training taught him how to efficiently kill the enemy in "hundreds of ways." He then testified that he had done his job well. His subdued voice got progressively louder. There seemed to be a need to purge his conscience. Although this drug-induced confession may have been good for his soul, it was upsetting to those still addressing their dinner plates. Somewhere in the one-sided dissertation, he mentioned that his best friend, Neil, had stolen his girlfriend, Joan, and "he'll pay for it." By the end of the cup of coffee, he was boisterously asserting his abilities to tear a man's heart out while it was still beating in his hands! With that proclamation, I found one of his friends to take him back to camp. For sure, it wasn't Neil. When Jim left that night there was nothing left. His eyes were vacant, and his head was as empty as a carved-out halloween pumpkin.

Jim touched me deeply, but I can't exactly say how. One morning two weeks later, an old beat-up Ford Pinto drove slowly by me in the Forest Service compound. The car then stopped, and Jim labored out of the passenger seat onto the gravel driveway, walked back, and shook my hand. "My friends have come to take me home. Thank you." He got back into the aging vehicle which, to my surprise, Neil was driving. They drove off. I never saw any of them ever again.

By the end of the 1979 season, the decision to move on was the logical next step in the evolutionary process of growth. I had met my lifemate, survived a life-threatening truck accident, and faced many gut-wrenching truths about myself during this four-year relationship with the wilderness. There is an energy that exudes from the unspoiled corners of earth's most perfect recesses, and I had spent my time there seeing and feeling what most people miss in life.

The snow had begun to accumulate by late November, and the trees were draped in the innocent white of serene and quiet bliss. Two days before my final departure, the word came from somewhere in western Washington that Jim had shot Neil to death and burnt his body along with the house in which they all had been living. It had been well over a year since I watched them drive away together. Upon comprehension of this message, the cold, stark beauty of my winter wonderland transformed into an icy void. There are some things in life you'd like to have remain the same forever, and my enchanting memories of the Lochsa would have been one of them. While selfishly lamenting this unlikely conclusion to a period that had touched my life with significance, my thoughts turned to Jim and the war he continues to fight. Maybe Jim was an eternally evil person predisposed to kill someone from the moment of birth. If that were so, I sure missed it. Ultimately, I came to this area to make sense out of the tumultuous times spawned by the hateful war I never had to fight. This was not the honorable war of our fathers, for it had nothing to do with a noble cause. The timing of this ironic news served as a swift kick back to a reality I now felt more competent to face. For some, that war will never end, and its effects will ripple through time. Count Jim, Neil, and everyone who knew them among the ongoing victims of an era when the mongers of greed dictated the most callous perpetrations upon its people while breaching the deep-seated trust of every individual. I can only hope there is a cosmic justice system.

Except for the veins of ice water that connected its well-placed pools, the Lochsa River had frozen over by the day of my departure. I stood and watched in the silence of an impending storm. Even out of that desolate gloom, I knew the cutthroat would survive to rise again for someone's well-placed fly when summer returned to this high country land of wonders, but I also knew it wouldn't be for mine. Still, winter represented the least of their worries. I learned much about life's imperfections from my perfect friends hidden in the waters below the ice, and that's what I took with me the day I drove down Highway 12 for the last time.

A year later I got this letter scrawled on a scrap sheet of paper:

Jerry-

Life has been a blurred checkerboard since I last saw you at the Lochsa Lodge.

Got committed to the nut house in October. Escaped—went to court—released. Picked up halloween for DUI and possession. Postponed to January. November arrested for the premeditated murder of Neil. I think he made a fatal mistake messing with the woman I love.

I expect to be out of here before Christmas time. May-be. Not guilty by reason of temporary insanity. A crime of passion by a hot blooded man. I was totally wasted and sleepless that A.M. and my ex said at the pre-trial that she saw the whole macabre affair!

Wish I could go back and untie that Gordian knot but I didn't tie it—he did!

Cross the River Styx and into Hades for another lost soul. Burn Baby Burn.

> *Have a nice Christmas*
> *Jim*

P.S. Thanks for the ride that nite—

Maybe I did miss something. But, for some reason, I found myself reaching for my guitar and singing the words of the late folk singer, Phil Ochs, whose songs in the late sixties vehemently protested the war:

> *Show me a prison, show me a jail,*
> *Show me a prison man whose face is growing pale*
> *And I'll show you a young man with many reasons why*
> *There but for fortune may go you or I.... you or I!*

Sometimes...
It all makes me wonder.

New Frontier

The earth I tread on...is not a dead, inert mass; it is a body, has spirit, is organic, and fluid to the influence of its spirit, and to whatever particle of that spirit is in me.

Henry David Thoreau

In Wisdom, Montana, there are two seasons—they say—winter and the fourth of July. Where I live in Twin Bridges, it isn't quite that bad; but the semi-blizzard and several days of north winds this week had me checking the calendar. Yup, it was the last week of May, and according to my calculations we were well into the ninth month of winter—although it even seemed longer than that. The cold and associated snow started sometime last September and it continued to hang on like a rabid pit bull. But not to worry, things were about to change. In a few days I was headed on my annual June excursion, a trip designed to shed the malaise brought on by too many months of stark landscapes, bare trees, and brutal reality.

From this standpoint, most folks would understand a journey that included places like the Florida Keys, the Bahamas or Belize, but unquestionably my intentions to return to Buffalo, New York, at this time of year raises some serious doubt about the soundness of my mind amongst friends and acquaintances. What about the salmon flies on the Big Hole, colleagues ask, or the green drakes at Henry's Fork? Albeit good inquiries, the increased numbers of anglers crammed into those legendary rivers in search of these often elusive hatches left me longing for alternatives several seasons ago. With so many other Western rivers flowing high and brown due to rain and melting snow, options are few at this time of year; that is, unless you are willing to travel. And for me, it's the Buffalo shuffle. So, while my friends express concern in a chorus of head scratching, a smile erupts as I drive off into the eastern sunrise.

But why Buffalo, you might ask—the city that's still trying to dig out of the 1977 blizzard, the city that lost four straight Super Bowls, the city often used by Jay Leno and David Letterman for comic relief in between the guffaws generated by their take on the most recent escapades of a political buffoon? When one throws in the fact that President William McKinley was assassinated there, Lake Erie once died on its doorstep, and its major sports legend, O.J. Simpson, was tried for a grisly double murder, no wonder the city is thought of as the Devil's Triangle of the north.

Consider also the image its inexplicable name conjures. As free as the wind swept the plains of Oklahoma, the bison once roamed North America by the millions until the early pioneer decided to systematically exterminate them, fueling an attitude that lives on to this very day. The new frontier was subdued, tamed and vanished with the buffalo. Even now, the few thousand that still wander the wilds of Yellowstone National Park are targeted by gun happy Montana whenever one dares to stray within its border. In what has to be considered one of the all-time great ironies, cows have readily replaced these massive beasts, once the embodiment of the very precepts of freedom upon which our country was firmly established. Even so, one can understand the association with Buffalo, Wyoming or South Dakota, but somehow Buffalo, New York, stretches the imagination. Then there's "Buffalo Bill" Cody who was attributed with leading the infamous buffalo slaughter of the 1800s, and now his name is immortalized by the city's professional football team.

Undoubtedly, the coordinates upon which this municipality stands do seem to fall squarely on the black hole of cruel fate. But to a privileged few, the city's much maligned and misunderstood character only serves to conceal a hidden world known to those who believe in another standard of importance. For beyond the exterior of inner city woes and haunting rusted factories lies an astonishing fact. It is not that the temperature rarely gets over ninety degrees there in the summer or below zero in the winter, it is not that one can still drive through the city during rush hour in less than a half hour or that the view of Lake Erie from the observation deck of city hall is truly breath-taking, but it *is* that Buffalo is likely the epicenter for some of the best fly fishing opportunities on the entire continent.

Now before you think I have spent one too many days staring out my window this winter, do this simple hands-on experiment. Get a map of North America and cut out the state of Montana. Then take the clipped image and paste it over the eastern portion of the country using Buffalo as the approximate center. Within the same geographical area that Montana covers you will notice that parts of Michigan, southern Ontario, Ohio, northern Pennsylvania, most of New York and three entire Great Lakes are engulfed. From the Delaware River in the Catskills to Letort Spring Run in Pennsylvania over to the Au Sable River in Michigan, blue ribbon trout fisheries abound within a Montana style drive from Buffalo. Then consider the quality fisheries offered by many Great Lakes tributaries within a short jaunt from the city. These include bountiful numbers of steelhead and salmon, huge brown trout, and the rare opportunity to catch lake trout on a fly. Add to the inventory an unparalleled smallmouth fishery found in Lake Erie along with the chance to encounter record fly rod muskellunge in the waters of the Niagara, and the possibilities are limitless. This list doesn't even include the endless numbers of lakes, rivers, and ponds throughout the entire area, which offer panfish of all shapes and sizes. Expand the horizons a bit and you'll find Atlantic salmon available in Quebec while abundant striped bass opportunities abound throughout the entire length of the eastern seaboard. When compared to the relatively short fishing season available in the Rockies and the hard-to-get-to aspect of Alaska, the easily accessible, year round opportunities within a prolific circle of Buffalo add up to world class status. So while it is true that I regularly return to visit my family in Western New York, it is also true they would likely see much less of me if they lived in Wichita, Kansas, or Lubbock, Texas.

But trying to shed the nefarious veil associated with the dark years of dead water has been a difficult challenge for the entire Great Lakes region, much less for Buffalo, with its perpetual cloud of gloom rivaled only by the one dangling atop the head of Charlie Brown. Then there is the matter of population. The swarm that dwells from the northeast back toward Chicago is difficult to ignore, and worse, some individuals reflect the disposition spawned by the years of dismal ignominy and loss of harmonious contact with the natural world. After all, behaviorists will point out, people are essentially products of their immediate environment.

But when one considers that the beautiful words of Henry David Thoreau were enlivened by the woods of New England and the thoughts of conservationist Aldo Leopold emerged from the wilds of Wisconsin, I find myself looking beyond the obvious deterrents to catch a glimpse of what these great visionaries once saw throughout this entire section of the continent. Too, the works of Robert Traver emanated from his fishing experiences of Michigan's upper peninsula, and even Ernest Hemingway wrote reverently about the Lake Superior region. Among the many others who seemed consumed by the vibrant uniqueness of the region was renowned naturalist and bird artist Roger Tory Peterson, whose work is recognized around the world. Taken all together, one gets the impression that below the surface there lies a tarnished jewel. And now that the Great Lakes have been restored in vast measure, it just may be that getting in touch with vestige remnants of these bygone inspirations is a real possibility. So it was for me this past summer, a rare chance to revisit a road I chose not to travel over a quarter century ago.

In Lake Erie the Canadian bass season starts a few weeks later than the American opener. As long as I can remember, it has always been so. The day was hot, still, and sultry as my brother Rick glided his sixteen foot Mirrocraft atop the billowy smooth surface of the lake. He has been running these waters for two decades, and we have been sharing angling adventures even longer than that. When all else fails, smallmouth fishing is our ace in the hole. This year we needed it. And since it was opening day in Canada, we headed for the waters that border Ontario.

To this point warm temperatures and the general lack of rain disrupted our normal June routine. Although local water-starved streams like the Wiscoy and Oatka provided spotty hatches for difficult wild browns, day trips to Ontario's Grand and Credit Rivers were fruitful, as was the two-day whirlwind to the Delaware. But other destinations were scratched as we learned of the unusual conditions that persisted throughout the entire Northeast and Midwest. While heavy rains flooded Michigan's Muskegon River and drought covered all of Pennsylvania, reports from the Matapedia in Quebec were of low, clear water and very few salmon. But when the stripers had mysteriously failed to arrive in the Kennebec within the time frame we had allotted, our disappointment was overwhelming. Since flexibility has always been our motto, when friend and striper guide Mike Augat delivered the bad news from his home in Maine, we realized that the only option was to forego the long drive and dig deeper into our bag of tricks.

Upon reaching the series of reefs and schoals Rick had in mind for our first stop, there were already a few boats spread out over a considerably large area. But they soon left, so we fished alone. The water was clear, no longer the color of a catfish pond as it had been when I grew up. It was so crystalline, in fact, that the visibility would have been over thirty feet if we weren't sitting just ten to fifteen feet above the rock-strewn basement of this massive freshwater impoundment. The pull of the Niagara River gently sucked us in the direction of the Peace Bridge as Erie's contents narrowed and formed the beginnings of the upper river in a violent protest of turbulence just a few miles away. The morning light painted the lake's floor. An underwater mural slowly passed below us—moonscape of rocks, depressions, and shadows hiding fish of various shapes and sizes. Standing watch in the backdrop on the southeast shore was the city of Buffalo, appearing like a giant poster hanging from a wall that subtly blended into the soft tones of a blue sky. Amidst the lineup of buildings proudly stood the paragon of the skyline, the historical thirty-story city hall, and with it, the memory of a much younger man.

Starting in 1972 and continuing on for nearly two years, I hung from almost every nook and cranny of the city's landmark working for a company that contracted to clean the envelope of industrial age grime from its huge blocks of sandstone. The union steward on the job was my sister's husband. Although he was also the crew chief, he played no favoritism. To prove the point, on my the very first day he stuck me on a movable lift outside the thirteenth floor with a guy wo had just been released from prison for killing someone in a bar room brawl. But my brother-in-law wasn't totally heartless, either. He assured me that I'd probably be all right as long the ex-con didn't have a drink.

My teaching position in Utah during the late sixties was then behind me, and the subsequent need to pay the bills required desperate measures. Suspended precariously from age-old outcroppings on a two-man scaffold paid top dollar, but the view of the world from such an extreme perspective was priceless. Regularly buffeted by winds that worked up a horrid frenzy over the open water, I would often gaze upon Lake Erie. Since this was the era when one of its tributaries in Ohio caught on fire, I was overwhelmed by the devastation. It seemed that I could only wish for bygone days when the lake was a vigorous body of water, fresh and alive—days that were never meant for my eyes. The reclamation of the Great Lakes had barely begun then, and word of rebounding fish populations were but an incomprehensible fantasy. My brother-in-law, along with the rest of the family, had hoped the job would help stake a new life for me in Western New York. But after every one of those blocks of sandstone was transformed from soot black to a crisp, natural tone of brownish tan, I pointed my restless being in the direction of the setting sun and drove toward it.

My move back West was as much an escape from the destructive forces that brought the East to its knees as it was to experience the rare essence of unrestrained wilderness and wide-open spaces. But now that the same debilitating forces have begun to dismantle the western third of the country, I find myself driven to rediscover the fragments of repose rising above the ashes of former transgressions in the East. Since we have filled up the land with our living just about everywhere, the truth is that we have to look for respite in the discarded corners of what is left. Because true wilderness is getting harder and harder to find, let alone reach, our only hope to find tranquility and peace in natural experiences is in the snippets that remain here and there. For the open minded, a change in attitude may unlock some worthwhile potential.

This, I believe, is the secret Buffalo hides today. Yes, some incredible fly fishing opportunities can be found in all directions, but I treasure much more. When I see a pair of wood ducks explode from a slough adjacent to Wiscoy Creek or watch a yellow-bellied sapsucker alight softly within a wooded edge along the Delaware, I make no judgments. Absorbed in a timeless interval that encompasses my entire being, the fibers of my soul, consumed by the powers of the great universe, transcend the mundane world. The one axiom found in all my travels is that emotional, spiritual, and creative survival for many, including myself, is intrinsically linked to contact with nature. Thus, wherever the road leads in search of fish, it also provides the ideal occasion to interact with all-important matters of the earth, and ultimately, life itself.

Undoubtedly, so many Eastern fishing options are alluring. But for me, it's about so much more. I desire to resurrect dreams that were effectively snuffed out in the dark ages of the Great Lakes. A fish is an object of mystery as well as an indicator of the health of what we can't see. That so many wonderful places for fish exist throughout the entire region these days has to mean something. I'd like to believe, at least in my case, the pursuit of fish, from trout to pike, is merely an excuse to explore the covert reaches of these surroundings for lost insights. A fetish with fins, these creatures provide a prayer-like pipeline to a higher order, a direct circuit to that which nourishes the inner self. Though no longer pristine, what the East has to offer is not without value. In fact, I embrace the rebirth. Considering the impaired environment which prevails throughout most of the country, it would seem that the *new frontier* of the technological age is to redefine our relationship with Earth's reclaimed niches in such a way that they are never squandered again.

So there I was, about to cast a fly into the water that I had abandoned so many years ago. Rick chose a Clouser's minnow for himself. For a bit of variation, I tied on a brown woolly bugger. Not that this was a random selection. I have always had wonderful success with this "bugger" in many situations across the country, especially when tied with orange thread and reinforced with copper wire. It is a simple, but effective impressionist. When all the technicalities pertaining to tackle were finally addressed, we began to fish.

What happened next would have made a great show for TNN. We fished for seven hours, and countless bass of all sizes up to five pounds chased our flies. In a day that would have made Jimmy Houston green with envy, we landed smallmouth—one after another. Two, three, four at a time chased each offering. And though there were slow periods, we'd float continuously over schools that littered the lake's bottom. Only a fraction of the fish were interested in our flies. Roland Martin would have flipped his stick. We quit when we couldn't cast our sink tips anymore, and we basked in the reality that we had found one of those discarded corners of reclaimed wonders. Easily, it could have been two hundred years ago. The parade of boats in the deeper channel faded into a hypnotic backdrop of non-existence. These days it is essential that you create your own illusion of open space.

Not too long ago the main criteria for judging the quality of the Western outdoor experience was the general lack of crowds. But in recent years the issue has taken on a rather different perspective in light of the fact that our mobile society has discovered the West. In fact, for the first time ever, grassroots consensus groups are gathering in Montana to discuss how to deal with over-crowding on its high profile rivers. Although it is still quite possible to fish there in solitude, there have been occasions when I have found less crowded waters in New York. Times are changing, and learning to share will be critical to the survival of what we all hold dear. Even though there is really no excuse for over population, somehow we are all going to have to find a way to live with the six billion (and counting) other human inhabitants on our planet. To the degree that we all cultivate an appreciation of the islands of nature that surround us, it is to that degree we will preserve the elements needed to nurture the human soul. "When we see land as a community to which we belong," writes Aldo Leopold, "we may begin to use it with love and respect."

The problem is two-fold: preserving ecological sanctuaries while, at the same time, learning how to derive some sense of sanctity from them. As an angler, I can either bury my head in a quagmire of apathy, or lead the way inspiring the changes needed as a by-product of this endeavor. Hope is the beacon for all of us who fish. Without it, we'd be better served swilling beer in an air-conditioned bar. But this same driving tenacity for keeping the fly in the water should also compel those of us who are serious anglers to do what it takes to help the rest of humanity balance the need of progress with the design of nature. The message is clear: take care of what is in our own backyards because there are very few places left for escape anymore. My annual trips to the East are a quest for rediscovery. I became keenly aware of the natural process, or the lack of it, when Lake Erie died. Years later, in its recovery, I look for answers.

Of all the bass we caught that day, I took one back with me. But only as a memory. Out of the past, just a few fish rise above the rest with the magic of a first kiss. Closing my eyes, the first wild steelhead still glistens in the golden stipples of October light on Idaho's Salmon River, while my first Atlantic salmon dances like a silver ghost in the fading shadows of an evening rain on the Margaree in Nova Scotia. And though this one bass was not my first, it does take its position in the line of piscatorial memories that meant much more than just catching a fish.

We saw the four-pounder glued to the rock shelf, a motionless figure that passed beneath the lazily drifting craft, but remaining acutely visible from the bow when the sun's rays were to our backs. My first instinct was to flip the woolly bugger on the water above it with the deftness of a Bassmaster. Immediately, from its position ten feet below, the fish rose exquisitely to inhale the appealing inducement. Only after it was quickly released did I draw comparison to the first westslope cutthroat I had ever caught on a dry fly in the waters of northern Idaho. From a deep pool of resplendent purity, the native trout lifted slowly upward until every detail became precisely revealed just before it took the floating coachman in a defining moment that lingers to this day. As that very cutthroat came to symbolize the reasons I moved West, this bass answered something deep inside me which became clear only when I glanced back upon city hall. From high upon its walls the spirit of the man I was twenty-seven years ago looked out upon a lake full of emptiness. The man I was now, however, just realized that the wish I made then had been granted this very day. In my lifetime, Lake Erie had once again become a vibrant body of water.

It would be difficult to conjecture what Thoreau and Leopold, or Muir, Emerson and the many other contemplative esthetes from the past would think of today's world. As disquieting as it may be, these writers were driven by their thoughtful expressions to promote the ideals of environmental soundness as a benchmark to measure how far the complex interaction of Earth and its inhabitants have strayed from the fundamental center of balance. In this same spirit, the modern outdoor writer should likewise try to raise the consciousness of as many individuals as possible— one reader at a time. Although it is an easy target to focus on present threats to the Earth's well being, it is also imperative to offer glimmers of hope demonstrating that some problems can be resolved. Otherwise, the task would be far too overwhelming.

When it comes to Buffalo, I preach my affection for this part of the country despite its less than noble past. Because of what the area wasn't when I was growing up, I chose a circuitous path of wondrous exploration that eventually led back to it. The rejuvenated Buffalo area touches my heart like no other place could ever do. I can see the mountains from my home in Montana, and they are beautiful beyond the words to describe them. But of all the roads traveled and rivers fished, the only move I would ever consider would be a return to Western New York.

For obvious reasons, my passion for the bison goes back to childhood. As for what this creature symbolizes, it would be difficult for any one of us to imagine the grief endured by the Indians of the Great Plains as the animal bearing the very soul of their culture was purposely wiped off the face of the earth. In the end, all that remained for these Native people were dead buffalo. And though it was this same pioneer "spirit" that continued to kill, cut down, and rearrange an awe inspiring land long before the profound consequences of these actions were ever realized, the damage to the East had begun long before spreading westward. Consequently, by 1960 all that remained for the people of Buffalo was a dead Lake Erie. What's in a name? It does make one wonder.

On my drive back to Montana, I saw a hanging sign with the two words "white buffalo" inscribed in hand painted letters. Bleached and barely visible on the skewed, weathered board, it seemed attached only by one remaining nail onto the side of a dilapidated building. Having some idea of what the white buffalo meant to the Plains Indian, I became consumed by the concept of this mysterious figure as I crossed South Dakota. By the time Rapid City came into view, I felt compelled to understand the significance of this image that filled my thoughts for hours.

Looking for insights in unusual places, I stopped at a mall alongside the interstate to search through a few bookstores for information to satisfy my burning curiosity. Finding nothing, I resolved that a library would likely be the best place to continue the investigation. Upon leaving the mall, I sensed an urge to enter one particular boutique for a final stop. Within a single step over the threshold I felt a strange enticement. In fact, within an instant I had crossed into a charismatic dimension of enchantment. The shop was filled with Native American charms and curios. Dream catchers and other feathered objects filled the closest corner.

Immediately, however, my eyes were drawn to the far wall. Hanging there were many beautiful paintings. Some were mystical Indian abstracts; many others were of free roaming bison wandering the imaginary plains of canvas. And then, in the middle of them all, there *it* was. The object of my quest: a beautiful oil depicting a white buffalo calf feeding on its mother's milk. The piece was entitled "The Sacred One."

A chill ran down my spine. Just then the artist appeared from behind a partition and proceeded to introduce himself. His name was Del Iron Cloud. We chatted for awhile. As an interpretive artist of the Lakota Sioux culture, his paintings are acclaimed throughout the country. In a positive sort of way, I felt guided by a force that was far beyond my control. The middle-aged Iron Cloud was tall and lean, his long-flowing, black hair swept back into a pony tail. Wearing a cowboy hat with a band of distinctive beadwork, the wisdom in his eyes accented the solemnity of his demeanor. Recognizing the power of the moment, I looked at him and announced at the same time, "I came to learn about the white buffalo." He stood in silence, as if generations of his people were passing through a vision in his mind. Then Iron Cloud proceeded to tell me the mythical tale.

"Once upon an honorable past," he began, "a beautiful woman appeared to two young Sioux boys in the form of a white buffalo. But she was so attractive, as it happened, that one of the boys lusted after her. So upon his advance, she killed him—thus establishing the seriousness of her message. With that done, she then told the other boy to go and bring back his people to her. When they returned, the white buffalo lady preached to them the words of unity from which the tradition of the peace pipe evolved—inspiring a way to honorably deal with problems facing their nation. In her final statement, she talked of a day when she would return once again. At that time there would be a great unification of all peoples. Then, before leaving, she rolled upon the earth four times: changing from white to black to red to yellow and then to brown. As she walked off, her color turned back to white. The different colors were a symbol of the many changes the Sioux would have to endure until her next coming."

As Iron Cloud came to the end of his story, there was a power shortage in the mall. The lights flickered off. In total darkness he continued on, saying that many of his people believe the white buffalo born in Minnesota in 1996 was actually her return. Then, with the lights back on, he concluded by emphasizing that "his people are firmly convinced that the time for the unification is now at hand." To the Sioux, the message is clear: all peoples must work together in a spirit of peace to solve every social issue around the world and, equally important, we must all do what it takes to heal the wounded earth before it is too late to save it.

After thanking him, I bought a small original watercolor of a bison. Iron Cloud signed it. I then continued on—but in an altered state. As if touched by the Great Spirit, I was fixated on a singular thought. It was simple, but profound. The words soughed through the canyons of time in the gentle currents of wind that rustled across the ages. As if a chant of holy wisdom permeated the land, it reverberated throughout the recesses of my innermost being. "May the white buffalo roam through the hearts of us all," was the refrain that played like a beautiful song in that corner of consciousness where only the sweet sound of music can touch.

Later, in the neighborhood of Buffalo, South Dakota, I caught a few trout. I had dinner in Buffalo, Wyoming. And since I couldn't miss the one day of summer in Montana, I arrived home with time to spare. It was July third. Although the temperature fell to thirty degrees that night, at least it didn't snow.

Dream Keepers

The day was innocent, full of the fluttering glow of richly colored aspen quaking an autumn serenade to the Big Blackfoot River as its water gently meandered through the sunlit corridor of gold. It could have been today, it could have been forty years ago, and it was magical—a freeze frame in time. But a camera could never capture the true depth of this day's beauty, the writer's pen would certainly balk with words of inadequacy. This was the Montana of dreams as seen through the eyes of Dan Bailey or Bud Lilly, unfettered by pretenses, uncluttered by ambitions. It was that rare kind of day, one filled with past glory and future hope.

This day out on the Blackfoot was specially chosen, for on that night the movie *A River Runs Through It* premiered in Bozeman. It had been years since my last visit to this fabled river, though the waters of many others had passed through my life since those weekends of the late seventies. Perhaps the word of the Blackfoot's descent into, at best, mediocrity, thanks to years of heavy metal mining waste, influenced the hiatus between visits. But on that day, I was looking for more than fish. So, while the festivities kicked off the movie, I was alone on the river that was about to run clear out of Montana and through the lives of many Americans.

A friend and colleague who worked closely with Robert Redford on the film as a fly fishing advisor forecasted a major change in the fishing industry after its showing. Jerry Siem and I would converse regularly about the movie-making business from his perspective. Needless to say, I was thrilled to get an insider's glimpse, especially when I saw a couple of his suggestions come to life on the big screen. And, as if a portent of things to come, change arrived swiftly for Jerry. Rewarded with a bit part in the movie, a major rod designing opportunity at Sage came his way soon afterward.

Redford himself was privately concerned about the film's lasting impact on Montana, but honoring a commitment made to Norman Maclean, this man's touching story was told with respect and dignity. "The Movie," as it came to be known in fly fishing circles, has become synonymous with the popularization— or trivialization, according to some—of the sport since its debut. And maybe there was a correlation, or maybe it was pure coincidence, but Montana began to change. Like a pilgrimage to Lourdes in quest of a cure, many came to Montana's rivers in search of something. Whatever it was, the Movie has been given credit for sparking that interest. And though nearly a decade has passed since its premiere in Bozeman, years of retrospection still pinpoint the changes that have occurred in the Big Sky State back to that major motion picture event.

Although Maclean's novella was never intended to be a fly fishing story, much less a movie, the subsequent interest that it generated not only mainstreamed the quiet pursuit of a rather specialized following, but this new-found focus also provided an economic windfall to the fly fishing industry. Rising to the occasion, technological ingenuity generated abundant choices of every gismo and service needed for the newly converted flock to enjoy fly fishing success. But while businesses thrived, there were some who dared suggest that the point of the film surely had been missed.

Undoubtedly, the river that ran through the hearts of so many alerted a nation to the wonders of fly fishing for trout. But it was the intangible element between the lines of the story that was assuredly minimized when the bottom line of profit and loss was finally tallied. To some, but certainly not all, the movie defined fly fishing as way of life, possibly offering an unlikely alternative to self-discovery and a meaningful existence. All along the seasoned angler understood this notion without ever fully expressing it. And though most would never cast a line where there are no fish, many would readily admit it is more than fish they are trying to catch. If nothing else, it seems Norman Maclean's sensitive piece gave rise to new perspectives of a dimension hidden within the inner being of those who have been called at one time or another to explore the sanctity found in the holy kingdom of trout.

Without question, where the land, the sky, and the water meet, there exists the window that opens to a reality free from the backstabbing competition and politics of the so-called real world. While there are those entrenched in the belief that one can't achieve true success unless the challenges on the battlefield of life, business or otherwise, are conquered, it is precisely this attitude many flee to the rivers to escape. Thus, in the same way the Movie defined one man's personal struggle to deal with life and ultimately, ghosts from his past, the story came to symbolize how fly fishing can be the creative force that also weaves a thread of sense through our own hectic existences.

I've always been a proponent of holistic fishing to keep the mind, heart, soul, and body working together in harmonious union. In fact, there may be no better way to get in touch with oneself or to bond with friends or other family members. Perhaps psychologist and fishing writer Dr. Paul Quinnett sums it up best in his book *Pavlov's Trout*. At one point he suggests that some of the most well-adjusted people he has ever met are those who have included fishing as a regular part of their lives. If nothing else, it would seem the Movie set the example of how fly fishing can permeate our lives in the right sort of way. In an era where we hunger for a spirituality appropriate for our times, perhaps this form of involvement with the natural environment is the one constant that can keep the human spirit focused on the basic substance from which we all evolved.

When I recall that day on the Big Blackfoot, it was the solitude I remember most. Although my log tells me that over a dozen trout came to hand on that historic October first, not one specific fish comes to mind. Although I do remember that each of them took a hopper, I was surprised, however, at the lack of anglers. For some reason, I figured there would be many others casting

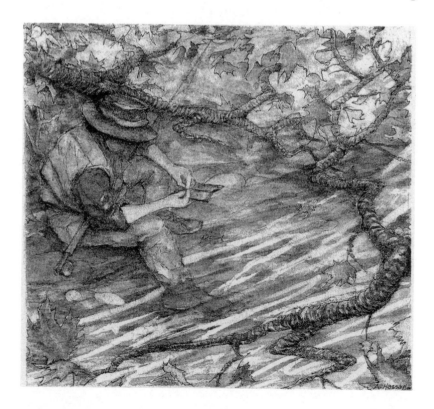

their line upon the water, looking for that same special something I was—trying to catch the essence of Maclean's story as it flowed through the rivulets that spanned the years. On that particular occasion, a symbolic gesture to the river seemed only fitting.

Don't get me wrong; I love to catch trout as much as anyone. And in order to enjoy fly fishing success on one level, it is necessary to learn the basic skills and understand the essential concepts. There are a host of books, schools, and willing experts available to accommodate those needs. But it shouldn't stop there. On another level, it is also very important to cultivate the right frame of mind. Likewise, there are an increasing number of publications, along with traditional literature, written to raise our consciousness, to open our minds and elevate our hearts to all the possibilities the total outdoor experience has to offer. With more and more folks looking for the same thing, how we approach the water, as well as the attitude we bring to it, will go a long way in defining the quality of the outing, the height of its enjoyment, and the depth of its significance.

Although wide open spaces, backwoods getaways, and secluded corners of the earth are more difficult to find nowadays, it is important to note that extracting value from being "out-a-doors" is still quite obtainable in the oasis provided by river corridors throughout the country. Solitude is often a state of mind. For instance, I have found solace on crowded eastern rivers when every one is mindful and respectful of each other. On the other hand, I have been crowded on empty western rivers when an irresponsible group of anglers have floated over a small patch of water I had been working for the evening. It is imperative to understand our obligation to tread lightly, especially on other individual's space.

Now for those who say all they want to do is " kick some serious fish butt," I am sure this book has fallen short in furthering those expectations. But catching fish becomes somewhat pointless if it is not considered an integral element of a broader scheme. So what I am suggesting here is a complete approach to our waters where the competitive, lip-ripping edge is left back in the fast lane of societal superficialities and the joyful spirit of camaraderie, sportsmanship, and involvement with nature are the main goals. Good fishing and personal fulfillment come only to those who have cultivated the necessary skills and proper disposition, and that all takes a commitment of time and devoted effort. If nothing else, the Movie made that point quite clear.

For those who have been called to this pursuit, there is a price to be paid if our trout rivers are to be sustained at the level capable of nourishing those who spend time on those waters. The complete angler should understand what this means. Throughout the nineties numerous problems have popped up on many of Montana's rivers. From whirling disease to dewatering and continuing siltation, the threats are real. Subdivision and development have channelized the Yellowstone, destroying critical trout habitat in the process. The proposed treated sewage release by a resort community into the pristine waters of the Gallatin River is yet another example of the hazards that imperil the trout's realm. Relentless forces they are, and once one fire is dealt with, another flares up somewhere else. Although we are all part of the problem to one degree or another, the solutions we seek will have to reflect our dedication to quality habitat, or it will be gone in short order. The track record is very clear in this regard. It is incumbent upon those of us who recognize the value of the outdoor experience to stand up for what we believe is important for the planet, and subsequently, for all of mankind. In the final analysis, the job of caretaking the rivers running through our lives does fall squarely upon all our shoulders.

As for the Big Blackfoot, much effort has been made to restore the river to its former prominence; but once lost, the road to recovery is tedious. And while one hand is tending to the effects of these past transgressions, the other has been planning another major gold cyanide heap leach mine in the upper reaches of the very river that has drawn all the attention to Montana. But the irony here has not slipped through the cracks of good sense and into the vast abyss of indifference. People are speaking out. The Movie inspired a legion of activists. Many folks throughout the country have come to the defense of the legendary river. Norman Maclean's famous final story line was as prophetic as it is intensely reflective. "I am haunted by waters," he solemnly concludes. These days, it would be for other reasons as well. In a way, we are all haunted by that which we love.

A friend of mine recently told me that when he steps into a river everything else melts into the background. Closing my eyes, I return to the day on the Big Blackfoot in 1992, and that experience melts into a perfect memory of what fly fishing should be about. For me, these days, it is more about giving back. If I could, I would pass on to future generations a world of rivers as important to them as they have been to me. The waters that adjoin us all over time should be more than a metaphor, but rather a shared vision kept alive by our unselfish passion to conserve and nurture the resource we have today for the benefit of those coming after us.

Whatever is important to the many who long for the magic of trout, whether it be the love of family and friends, the oneness with nature, the call of the wild or more, a river truly does run through it all. But responsibility is a cross we all must bear. And like it or not, we are the ones who will determine how the resources are maintained and, ultimately, how the sacredness of their spirit is preserved.

Eyes closed, illusions fill the gathering darkness. As reality merges with timeless fantasies, fading light dances to the mystical moods, a symphony of sound and silence, while consciousness drifts into oblivious serenity. The resounding water echoes the song of trout in that distant dream where all is one. Memories to savor, experiences to share. The legacy has been entrusted to those of us who have been called to the rivers.

Sentinels at the gate. The watch is ours. We are the dream keepers.

Arctic Flower

I don't know why I fish, let alone why I fish so much. Some may even think my passion is a bit misguided, a pathological addiction that serves no purpose save for the fitful avoidance of life's many trials and tribulations. But after years of self-evaluation, I prefer to believe there is more to my chosen lifestyle than the wayward meandering of an unholy soul. My quest for one more cast on one more river has always been accompanied by the desire to seek answers to that which I cannot understand. Partially submerged in water, I do not avoid, but rather see more clearly beyond the undefined shadows that shape the existence to which we all belong.

From the moment I first read Joe Brooks, the path has been clear. For close to thirty years I have been true to my goal; yet there are so many more rivers, and so little time. Recently, the journey passed through the High Arctic in pursuit of the elusive char, a fish that dwells in a vast region of unfathomable harshness. Though a summer on the tundra is seductively deceptive, the tantalizing lull of constant daylight serves only as brief respite from the absolute power that fills the remainder of the year. Even the curious eyes of the muskox, a throwback beast with remarkable survival skills, seem to reflect an abiding respect for this land of raw force. Most of us could never imagine the elements these unique creatures endure. As for the object of my pursuit, the first Arctic char I ever caught was huge. While admiring the subtle beauty of this uncommon ocean dweller before its release, I trembled as if I were embracing the very soul of the Arctic in my hands, a gift of awesome proportions.

Suquamish leader Chief Seattle once stated that "the earth does not belong to us, we belong to the earth." It would then seem no coincidence that many holy men throughout the ages retreated at times to the wilderness to contemplate this belonging. Often these sage beings emerged with visions of truth. And though lifestyles have changed these days, something doubtlessly gnaws at the core of a restless society, as if the need to be drawn into the bosom of Mother Earth is still in our genes. Because it was difficult not to, I spent time in the Arctic contemplating the magnitude of our insignificance on a land of unabashed austerity. Rivers and wild places—a simple concept. Could this be the panacea for all that ails the human psyche? I concluded that if I were to write a modern Bible upon my return from the wilderness, it would consist of one sentence: Respect yourself, every person, every creature, and especially the earth to which we all belong— the rest will fall into place.

The night before I departed for the Arctic, I bought some ice cream at our local pizza parlor. A young gal with a friendly smile served me. I casually paid her, and then was on my way. Less than twelve hours later this beautiful child was killed in a car wreck. It is a thing like this that I do not understand. Although I didn't know her, a small town is like an extended family. Everyone mourns the loss of its own, and all suffer grievously. Someone's daughter, gone. Pain beyond comprehension. I left town an hour after hearing the devastating news.

Later that week, in the soft glow of the midnight sun, I picked an Arctic flower and placed it on the flowing water of the Nanook

River. In her memory I watched the petals of white ride the riffles and rivulets of time until the offering disappeared into eternity, embraced by the sacred water of the Arctic char. There was little else I could do. But then, that's how I deal with life.

In solemn silence, alone I stood.

Once again, at the river's edge.